Into Solution

Daily Support for Recovery Treatment Center Staff

Compiled by

Mary Crocker Cook

Into Solution

© 2015 Mary Crocker Cook

ISBN: 978-1-61170-201-9

Published by:

 Robertson Publishing™
www.RobertsonPublishing.com

Printed in the USA and UK on acid-free paper.
To purchase additional copies of this book go to:
amazon.com
barnesandnoble.com

Other titles by Mary Cook:

Awakening Hope. *A Developmental, Behavioral, Biological Approach to Codependency*

Afraid to Let Go. *For Parents of Adult Addicts and Alcoholics*

Codependency and Men. *Where Early Attachment, Gender Role, and Adrenal Fatigue Meet*

Wake Them Up. *They'll Listen to You. Psychoeducation Strategies for Chemical Dependency Counselors. Co-author, Chris Packham.*

Welcome to My World. *(A novel) A week in the life of a substance abuse counselor.*

The Work Goes On. *(A Novel) Another week in the live of a substance abuse counselor.*

Don't Leave!!! *Codependency and Attachment*

This mediation journal is a labor of love. It is designed for personal use, counselor support groups, as well as counselor training.

I have spent 25 years working in the addiction field and educating addiction counselors. As much as I love the recovering addict, I love their counselors even more. Then again, they're usually the same people!

"Helping, fixing, and serving represent three different ways of seeing life. When you help, you see life as weak. When you fix, you see life as broken. When you serve, you see life as whole. Fixing and helping may be the work of the ego, and service the work of the soul."

Rachel Naomi Remen

It's a new year and a chance to recommit to balancing service to clients with self-care. This isn't always easy because client need is endless. In treatment we're surrounded by people raw with anxiety and we can get sucked into believing that NOT taking our vacation or working the extra hours will somehow contain the anxiety. Every client has a resilience they've forgotten, so it's important that we remember it! It's also important that we protect our own resilience because we have another whole year ahead of us!

_____

_____

_____

_____

_____

_____

_____

_____

_____

_____

_____

_____

_____

January 2 — Patterns

"I truly believe we can either see the connections, celebrate them, and express gratitude for our blessings, or we can see life as a string of coincidences that have no meaning or connection.

For me, I'm going to believe in miracles, celebrate life, rejoice in the views of eternity and hope my choices will create a positive ripple effect in the lives of others. This is my choice."

Mike Ericksen, Upon Destiny's Song

Part of the art of counseling is our ability to see pattern in seemingly random behaviors. It's this objective witness of a client's story that allows us to draw attention to their patterns in a way that gives them a choice to change them. As helpers we have the same opportunity to find a non-judgmental witness in our own lives that can help up untangle behaviors we can't see to change. We all have blind spots!

_____
_____
_____
_____
_____
_____
_____
_____
_____
_____
_____
_____
_____

JANUARY 3 — SELF-ACCEPTANCE

"Self-love isn't always so poetic; sometimes it's a nice big triple back flip kick in the ass. You've got to call yourself on your own nonsense; on the incredibly efficient way you can be self-destructive."

Steve Maraboli

I love this quote—it made me laugh out loud! It's so true that our own personal growth can be a messy affair. Even if we have years of recovery, we still often have our self-doubt and self-criticism sneak out in self-destructive ways. It peeks out in the extra piece of cake we don't need, tolerating poor behavior from others in our personal life, or martyring ourselves at work. Self-destruction can be sneaky. When we tell on ourselves, and hold ourselves in loving accountability, there's hope!

_____
_____
_____
_____
_____
_____
_____
_____
_____
_____
_____
_____
_____
_____
_____
_____

January 4 — Self-Compassion

There is that part of ourselves that feels ugly, deformed, unacceptable. That part, above all, we must learn to cherish, embrace, and call by name.

MacRina Wiederkehr, A Tree Full of Angels

It's my experience that people who choose the helping profession frequently have very high standards for ourselves. We can lack compassion with our inadequacies and imperfection. All traits have a positive and negative aspect, so every aspect of us is valuable.

For example:
- Stubbornness: Can get you to a goal, can keep you from a goal.
- Generosity: Can help people grow or enable their disease.
- All parts of you are necessary and valuable. Maybe it's worth getting to know you better!

January 5 — Loving the Unlovable

When we attempt to clear up the mess others have made, or when we love the unlovely, we demonstrate the kind of weirdness God likes. We give the lie to the evolutionary survival of the fittest maxim..."

> Ann Benton, *If It's Not Too Much Trouble:*
> *The Challenge of the Aged Parent*

Many of us have a gift for loving the unlovable, and it's this unique heart that led us to choose a helpers path. In fact, this trait may also be our downfall because we have not loved ourselves enough, and tolerated the intolerable too often. Our compassion reminds us that we've exhibited unlovable behavior in our disease or in moments of anger and frustration. Seeing through the behavior into a client's heart is our gift and is the source of our compassion.

_____
_____
_____
_____
_____
_____
_____
_____
_____
_____
_____
_____
_____
_____

It's no accident that most self-help groups use 'anonymous' in their names; to Americans, the first step toward redemption is a ritual wiping out of the self, followed by the construction of a new one.

Walter Kirn

Many of us had to experience the death of who we've been in order to be who we are now. The ego doesn't disappear willingly; it fights, scrambles, bargains, rages. We only surrendered our egos because we had to, we were desperate to change and allowing an alternative version of ourselves to emerge was the only way we were going to survive. We change when the stakes are high enough. What makes our work interesting is that the tipping point is different for every client. It gives us compassion and a sense of humor when we reflect on how hard we had to hit our heads before we were willing to change!

_____
_____
_____
_____
_____
_____
_____
_____
_____
_____
_____
_____
_____

January 7 — Detachment

"All I'm saying is that I want you to be happy. I don't care how it happens, or what it takes to facilitate it. I don't care if it happens with me or without me. I don't care if you use me to get there, or if I'm entirely irrelevant to your process. None of me is attached to how your happiness happens; I care only that it does."

Agnostic Zetetic

We can begin to invest a lot pride in our work with others, and begin to overestimate our influence on the change process. We begin to want to be the "source" of healing which can lead us to believe WE are the client's Higher Power. We need to keep the end in mind without having to control the process, and ultimately it's a healthy recovery for those we serve. This may mean we are entirely dispensable in the process, and this as it should be. It's their journey.

January 8 — Self-Compassion

"I am my own biggest critic. Before anyone else has criticized me, I have already criticized myself. But for the rest of my life, I am going to be with me and I don't want to spend my life with someone who is always critical. So I am going to stop being my own critic. It's high time that I accept all the great things about me."

C. JoyBell C.

Why do we believe self-criticism is helpful? Some of us act as if we can only be motivated by a kick in the ass—that if we aren't hard on ourselves we'll be "slackers." What if there's a middle choice—self-discernment along with self-compassion as a path to growth. Being honest about ourselves through a kind lens, a lens that recognizes we're human, is ultimately going to be more effective. Christopher Germer says, *"A moment of self-compassion can change your entire day. A string of such moments can change the course of your life. "*

_____

_____

_____

_____

_____

_____

_____

_____

_____

_____

_____

_____

January 9 — Self-Discovery

"I feel very privileged to hear how somebody used to run around stickin' people up and stealing cars, and now they're gettin' their life back together... I just love the stories. The stories of the fallen world, they excite us. That's the interesting stuff."

Denis Johnson

It's tempting to get lost in the content of a client's story, the "Jerry Springer" drama. Chaos can be seductive and can even bring back old memories of our own wild times. The goal is to assist the client to begin to see self-discovery and life on life's terms as interesting and compelling. The prospect of a future, a future based in reality has its own wildness, its own challenge, and can make recovery equally seductive. Do you find your own life compelling, or are you losing yourself in theirs?

_____
_____
_____
_____
_____
_____
_____
_____
_____
_____
_____
_____
_____
_____

"When you judge other people without wanting to know the true story behind their actions, is usually when there is something inside of you that is so broken that if you found out what you believed about them was a lie, you wouldn't want to accept it or make amends."

Shannon L. Alder

We usually believe being snarky toward others is justified. After all, if I'm giving my husband the silent treatment or refuse to cover a co-worker's shift because I judged them to be a "lazy-ass," I might even have a nice ripple of self-satisfaction. Most of the time people who irritate us have something to teach us about ourselves if we pay attention. Judgments about others are often reflections of a part of ourselves we are avoiding. Irritating people can be a mirror!

_____
_____
_____
_____
_____
_____
_____
_____
_____
_____
_____
_____
_____
_____

When I loved myself enough, I began leaving whatever wasn't healthy. This meant people, jobs, my own beliefs and habits—anything that kept me small. My judgment called it disloyal. Now I see it as self-loving.

Kim McMilllen

What's limiting you in your life? Do you have an imaginary ceiling on your career because you're afraid to go back to school? Maybe someone in your life is threatened by your desire to grow, and you're afraid to lose the relationship? There comes a point in our personal growth when we will have to tolerate the anxiety of change, recognizing that anxiety is part of growth, not an enemy to avoid at all costs. It's true that life is risky when you bet on yourself.

_____
_____
_____
_____
_____
_____
_____
_____
_____
_____
_____
_____
_____
_____
_____
_____
_____

"Your time is limited, so don't waste it living someone else's life. Don't be trapped by dogma — which is living with the results of other people's thinking. Don't let the noise of others' opinions drown out your own inner voice. And most importantly, have the courage to follow your heart and intuition. They somehow already know what you truly want to become. Everything else is secondary."

Steve Jobs

Are you operating out of an outdated belief system about yourself or the world around you? When we first get clean our world can be narrow to be manageable. It helps us keep our focus on our recovery. With time our recovery needs to expand, our worldview broaden as our tolerance and preconceived notions outgrow their usefulness. When was the last time you challenged your own assumptions and ideas?

_____
_____
_____
_____
_____
_____
_____
_____
_____
_____
_____
_____
_____
_____

January 13 — Scar tissue

"Our hearts will be broken a thousand times over, but who is to say that our hearts were ever perfect to begin with? Maybe they can withstand a few cracks. After all, the way that we love is not perfect. We love things to such an incomprehensible depth that these things become worn in. Wouldn't the most beautiful thing in the world be a heart that has been through all of the wear and tear, as worn in as your favorite sweater that both keeps you warm and grants you a smile in return? That's the kind of heart that I want. Bruises make for beautiful colors after all."

Elizabeth Brooks

Many of us bring hearts full of scar tissue which has softened us. While it is true pain can make some people harder, helpers have usually developed compassion as a result of their life experiences. The scar tissue lets us recognize the scars in our clients, and gives us patience with them when they're still acting out their pain. We've been there.

_____

_____

_____

_____

_____

_____

_____

_____

_____

_____

_____

January 14 — Going through the motions

"I was a little excited but mostly blorft. "Blorft" is an adjective I just made up that means 'Completely overwhelmed but proceeding as if everything is fine and reacting to the stress with the torpor of a possum.' I have been blorft every day for the past seven years."

Tina Fey, Bossypants

I immediately recognized the feeling, "torpor of a possum." For me this means I'm in suspended animation, going through the motions, and disconnected from myself. As helpers we need to carry energy into relationships with our clients, and notice when we're "phoning it in." We need to refill our emotional wells on a regular basis to have the vitality we need to make the difference in the lives of others we're capable of making.

_____
_____
_____
_____
_____
_____
_____
_____
_____
_____
_____
_____
_____
_____
_____
_____

"As I sit today, I am a genuine, often pleasant person. I am able to imitate a human being for long spurts of time, do solid work for a reputable organization, and have, over the breadth of time, proven to be an attentive father and husband. So how to reconcile my past with my current circumstances? Drugs, it seems to me, do not conjure demons, they access them. Was I faking it then, or am I faking it now? Which, you might ask, of my two selves did I make up?"

David Carr, The Night of the Gun

The truth is we all have a number of selves we bring out in a variety of circumstances. Sometimes we function like a responsible adult and sometimes we act like a 5 year old! This was true of us loaded or not. We all have parts of ourselves that we either access or ignore. If we ignore them for too long they can pop out and startle us – even cause chaos in our lives. The problem isn't our multiple facets, it's our lack of awareness.

_____

_____

_____

_____

_____

_____

_____

_____

_____

_____

_____

_____

January 16 — Resilience

"We've been there and come back. When you fall in the pit, people are supposed to help you up. But you have to get up on your own. We'll take your arms, but you have to get your legs underneath you and stand."

Bucky Sinister, Get Up: A 12-Step Guide to Recovery for Misfits, Freaks, and Weirdos

It's important to remember our role in the lives of our clients, and to recognize that their recovery is going to be a result of the work THEY put into the process. We have the chance to remind the clients of their strengths, their opportunities, their options. We can offer guidance, feedback, support. Ultimately, our clients have a decision to make about the course of their lives, and we cannot, and should not, make it for them.

"We must be content to grow slowly. Most of us will still barely be at the beginning of our recovery by the time we die. But that is better than killing ourselves pretending to be healthy."

Simon Tugwell

It's so hard to be patient with the pace of change in our lives. We can see the goal, yet forget to appreciate and be at peace with the process. This is especially true if we lost years of our lives to addiction, codependency, or depression and we're acutely aware of how much we want to make up for lost time. We can relate to our clients who want to have the rewards of years of recovery when they have 6 months clean. You can be a role model for patience with the process and treat yourself with kindness.

_____

_____

_____

_____

_____

_____

_____

_____

_____

_____

_____

_____

_____

_____

_____

_____

"Maybe you've gotten through something and when you did you thought, I am leaving that behind and will never return. And that's a great way of thinking...for selfish jerks.

If we actually care about people other than ourselves, we can't leave our problems behind and never return. If we don't take the freedom we've experienced and try to bring it to others, we are not becoming people worth becoming."

Vince Antonucci, Guerrilla Lovers: Changing the World
with Revolutionary Compassion

The majority of helpers working in chemical dependency treatment entered the field feeling a responsibility to share the compassion and kindness that has been extended to them. Service is key to our recovery, and it is not just our responsibility to give back but it's our privilege. Service changes us in ways we never expected.

_____
_____
_____
_____
_____
_____
_____
_____
_____
_____
_____
_____
_____
_____

"By honoring and responding to your natural and essential requirements for sleep, food, water and movement, you will rise out of the realm of survival into the world of fulfillment."

Miranda J. Barrett, A Woman's Truth: A Life Truly Worth Living

We often operate it the world as though we're a floating head, separate from the physical body that houses us. Our bodies and minds are intricately connected, and treating them as though they're separate allows us to neglect ourselves and deny the fatigue, sluggishness, stiffness that haunts us all day long. Addiction is a physical disease and we need to remind ourselves and our clients that our bodies deserve attention and the chance to heal. We need to treat our bodies with respect and give it the nutrition and movement it needs to support us in our work with others.

_____

_____

_____

_____

_____

_____

_____

_____

_____

_____

_____

_____

_____

_____

"The key problem I encounter working with wounded, depressed, and unhappy people is a lack of connection... starting from a disconnection from themselves and then with others. This is why love often becomes so distorted and destructive. When people experience a disconnection from themselves, they feel it but do not realize the problem."

David W. Earl

We can offer empathy and accurate emotional response when we recognize the emotional reality of others. We learned to do this by having our own emotional world reflected back to us by someone who could hear and see us accurately. Maybe it was a therapist, a sponsor, or a family member. Being connected with our own perceptions and reality supports us to connect with others and offer accurate and helpful observations. If you aren't hearing people well right now, maybe you need to be heard.

_____
_____
_____
_____
_____
_____
_____
_____
_____
_____
_____
_____
_____

How would your life be different if...You stopped allowing other people to dilute or poison your day with their words or opinions? Let today be the day...You stand strong in the truth of your beauty and journey through your day without attachment to the validation of others"

Steve Maraboli, Life, the Truth, and Being Free

Our co-workers have their own recovery process and struggles, and as a team member we value their input and observations about our performance. People who work in treatment vary in their levels of recovery and you may have co-workers that still struggle with judgmental and defensive behavior. Maybe they even direct their criticism toward you and take your inventory and this can be very disappointing. Recognize that our compassion for hurting people needs to extend to our coworkers for us to work together peacefully.

_____
_____
_____
_____
_____
_____
_____
_____
_____
_____
_____
_____
_____

JANUARY 22 — STAYING POSITIVE

To be hopeful in bad times is based on the fact that human history is not only of cruelty, but also of compassion, sacrifice, courage, kindness. If we see only the worst, it destroys our capacity to do something. If we remember those times and places where people have behaved magnificently, this gives us the energy to act. And if we do act, in however a small way, we don't have to wait for some grand Utopian future. The future is an infinite succession of presents, and to live now as we think human beings should live, in defiance of all that is bad around us, is in itself a marvelous victory.

Howard Zinn

We have daily reminders of the worst of people, as we're faced with the histories of those we serve — poor decisions and pain left in the wake of addiction. It would be easy to become cynical to protect ourselves. The harder path, the courageous path, is to stay aware of the goodness and grace life extends to us and through us.

January 23 — Planting Seeds

"Any ordinary favor we do for someone or any compassionate reaching out may seem to be going nowhere at first, but may be planting a seed we can't see right now. Sometimes we need to just do the best we can and then trust in an unfolding we can't design or ordain."

Sharon Salzberg

One of the more challenging aspects of counseling is the lack of immediate feedback. In fact, just when clients are beginning to be stable and fully participating in their own recovery they move on to the next level of care! So we frequently don't know the end of the book, and don't know if the people in whom we have invested our time and attention are still clean and successful. We need to remember that we are only part of the healing process, and every kindness, every insight you offer, matters.

_____
_____
_____
_____
_____
_____
_____
_____
_____
_____
_____
_____
_____
_____

January 24 — Acceptance

"To bow to the fact of our life's sorrows and betrayals is to accept them; and from this deep gesture we discover that all life is workable. As we lean to bow, we discover that the heart holds more freedom and compassion than we could imagine."

Jack Kornfield

So much of our suffering comes from our refusal to accept what we are facing. We bargain, try to reframe, negotiate, resist...anything but bow in surrender. I spent several years of my life this way, and the rigidity of the position I was taking made me ill. Life is fluid, gently and persistently moving forward regardless of how we feel about it. Our consent is neither required nor needed. Our job is to flow with it rather than be snapped in half by it.

_____

_____

_____

_____

_____

_____

_____

_____

_____

_____

_____

_____

_____

_____

_____

_____

"You are only plagued with stress in moments of conflict because you are arrogant, and believe others are transgressing by having unfavorable thoughts about you."

Bryant McGill, Simple Reminders

We can get so twisted in our attempts to control the impression others have of us. We work hard to create an impression of who we are, what we're about, and it can be a painful ego blow when someone challenges our image. We act out and feel outraged, misunderstood, and justify ourselves when we retaliate. Maybe they're seeing something about us that we need to acknowledge and manage more effectively. Ultimately it can be a relief to stop identifying with our image and relax into who we are.

_____

_____

_____

_____

_____

_____

_____

_____

_____

_____

_____

_____

_____

_____

_____

_____

_____

_____

"There is no social stigma attached to the frenzy, no peer motivation to slow us down. Rather it is the opposite; busy is popular currency, traded among members of modern society like a precious commodity. Busy is the silkiest cloth at the emporium, the most well-travelled spice. Living with a full schedule speedily typed into a pinging, vibrating device is a highly valued state of being. And, as with any addiction, it becomes self-perpetuating. We feel a rush from being in a rush; we take pride in the breakneck pace at which we travel through our days."

Gillian Deacon, Naked Imperfection: A Memoir

Unfortunately being busy can led us to believe that we're important, and we feel urgency about being connected, available, responsive. It's as though we're 4 years olds sneaking down the banister after bed time, afraid of missing something. We aren't missing anything if we turn the phone off, take a nap. In fact, we are gaining access to ourselves, which is precious.

_____

_____

_____

_____

_____

_____

_____

_____

_____

_____

_____

_____

"Your job is obviously very pressured."

"I thrive under pressure," I explain. Which is true. I've known that about myself ever since... Well. Ever since my mother told me when I was about 8.

Sophie Kinsella, The Undomestic Goddess

Some of us come to the helping profession with well-honed skills for chaos and unpredictability. Early in life we were providing emotional support to our parents, raising our younger siblings, handling financial crisis, and responding to violence. We're good at it, and forget that there's an alternative way to live our lives. We can develop skills to tolerate predictability, gentleness, and live our lives more easily with room for breathing.

_____
_____
_____
_____
_____
_____
_____
_____
_____
_____
_____
_____
_____
_____
_____

"When service is unto people, the bones can grow weary, the frustration deep. Because, agrees Dorothy Sayers, "whenever man is made the center of things, he becomes the storm-center of trouble. The moment you think of serving people, you begin to have a notion that other people owe you something for your pains"

Ann Voskamp, One Thousand Gifts: A Dare to Live Fully Right Where You Are

The nature of counseling requires our energy to go toward the client, and not only can they be ungrateful, but they can actively fight our attempts to help them. This can make us weary and resentful, and cause us to be short tempered with our clients and withhold our compassion since it seems "wasted" on them. Much like sponsorship, extending our compassion helps US stay focused on our own growth. It's worth the effort.

_____

_____

_____

_____

_____

_____

_____

_____

_____

_____

_____

_____

_____

"We talk about social service, service to the people, service to humanity, service to others who are far away, helping to bring peace to the world - but often we forget that it is the very people around us that we must live for first of all. If you cannot serve your wife or husband or child or parent - how are you going to serve society? If you cannot make your own child happy, how do you expect to be able to make anyone else happy? If all our friends in the peace movement or of service communities of any kind do not love and help each other, whom can we love and help?"

Thích Nhất Hạnh

We are being reminded to not extend all of our energy and patience at work. All too often those close to us get the "leftovers," when we are too exhausted to hear them. They deserve the best of us. Self-care gives us enough energy for everyone.

_____

_____

_____

_____

_____

_____

_____

_____

_____

_____

_____

_____

_____

JANUARY 30 — BOUNDARIES

"Many of us follow the commandment 'Love One Another.' When it relates to caregiving, we must love one another with boundaries. We must acknowledge that we are included in the 'Love One Another."

Peggi Speers

We teach our clients about boundaries all the time in treatment, and recognize that when they lose themselves they become vulnerable to relapse and codependency. What about our boundaries with our clients? When our internal boundaries are weak, we can get sucked in to the strong emotions and anxiety of those around us. We can take on the financial worry of the program owner, the fear of family members, or fatigue of coworkers. We need to be able to observe the concerns and worries of others without letting them become our reality.

_____

_____

_____

_____

_____

_____

_____

_____

_____

_____

_____

_____

_____

_____

January 31 — Head and heart

"Some people think only intellect counts: knowing how to solve problems, knowing how to get by, knowing how to identify an advantage and seize it. But the functions of intellect are insufficient without courage, love, friendship, compassion, and empathy."

Dean Koontz

We have so many clever clients, people who used their intelligence to manage access to their drugs, conned people out of money to support their need for alcohol, and talked their way out of consequences. We may have been this way in our own using! It can be exciting to introduce our clients to alternative uses for their intellect, and model the value and wisdom of compassion and empathy in our exchanges with them. Problems are best solved when we consult with the head AND heart.

"The most important reason for your "no" is that you need your downtime so you won't behave like a jerk because you're depleted. And you don't want to battle an appetite spiked by the stress of over commitment. But that's your secret; others don't need that information. So just smile, say no, thank you, and keep moving."

Holly Mosier

How aware are you of signs that you are becoming depleted. Are you irritable, sarcastic, avoidant, compulsively eating, or spending money unwisely? Even though someone may have resentment when you aren't immediately available, it's relationship preservation to take some time for yourself and offer your best to the people around you.

We became helpers to provide support and it eats away at our self-esteem when we catch ourselves acting unkindly toward towards our clients, and see the hurt and disappointment in their eyes. It hurts our heart to hurt theirs.

FEBRUARY 2 — COMPASSION

"Compassion asks us to go where it hurts, to enter into the places of pain, to share in brokenness, fear, confusion, and anguish. Compassion challenges us to cry out with those in misery, to mourn with those who are lonely, to weep with those in tears. Compassion requires us to be weak with the weak, vulnerable with the vulnerable, and powerless with the powerless. Compassion means full immersion in the condition of being human."

Henri J.M. Nouwen

If we're going to meet people where they are it means we have to have to be willing to enter the client's world. This requires courage on our part, because sometimes a client's world can be dark and full of trauma. We are there to bear witness to what they've been afraid to face on their own. We need to lend them our courage and to have our own support system to then heal us!

_____

_____

_____

_____

_____

_____

_____

_____

_____

_____

_____

_____

_____

FEBRUARY 3 — DESERVING

"Be kind to people whether they deserve your kindness or not. If your kindness reaches the deserving good for you if your kindness reaches the undeserving take joy in your compassion."

James Fadiman, Essential Sufism

I never know what to do with the word "deserving." I've heard it used to justify the withholding of love and opportunities so it's not a word I use very often. I suppose there are too many times I have not "deserved" the compassion I have received. Fortunately people in my life have been kind to me at times when I could not be kind to myself, and so it's possible for me to extend this same kindness. If you find yourself judging someone's deservingness, it's possible you need more kindness yourself.

"Even if toxic people are right about what is "good," they are wrong if the approach is not healthy."

John Lewis Land

How attached are you being "right"? Counselors can often get into unnecessary power struggles with clients in a conviction that they're right and the client needs to comply with the treatment plan the counselor has created for them. I've seen this with counselors who are convinced that their personal recovery program is the only valid path. It's important that we retain humility in the face of addiction, and that we, in fact, cannot know what's best for other people. We can only make suggestions . . . this is the attitude Bill Wilson emphasized as a result of his own efforts to force recovery on others!

_____

_____

_____

_____

_____

_____

_____

_____

_____

_____

_____

_____

_____

_____

_____

February 5 — Meaning

"There is a great difference between one idler and another idler. There is someone who is an idler out of laziness and lack of character, owing to the baseness of his nature. If you like, you may take me for one of those. Then there is the other kind of idler, the idler despite himself, who is inwardly consumed by a great longing for action who does nothing because his hands are tied, because he is, so to speak, imprisoned somewhere, because he lacks what he needs to be productive, because disastrous circumstances have brought him forcibly to this end. Such a one does not always know what he can do, but he nevertheless instinctively feels, I am good for something! My existence is not without reason! I know that I could be a quite a different person! How can I be of use, how can I be of service? There is something inside me, but what can it be? He is quite another idler. If you like you may take me for one of those."

Vincent van Gogh, The Letters of Vincent van Gogh

_____

_____

_____

_____

_____

_____

_____

_____

_____

_____

_____

_____

_____

"There is a fine line between compassion and a victim mentality. Compassion though is a healing force and comes from a place of kindness towards yourself. Playing the victim is a toxic waste of time that not only repels other people, but also robs the victim of ever knowing true happiness."

Bonnie Ware, The Top Five Regrets of the Dying: A Life Transformed by the Dearly Departing

It can be easy to cosign a victim story, particularly when it's a story we share. In fact being a victim may be a comfortable place for us, and we do our clients a disservice when we join them in their helplessness. Seeing our part of the problem gives us a realistic basis for hope because we can change our behaviors and make new decisions. Our part is our hope, not the focus of blame. Listen to your own "victim speak" as you go about your day and pay attention to the ways this kind if self-talk depletes you and strips your motivation.

"Diversity makes for a rich tapestry. We must understand that all the threads of the tapestry are equal in value, no matter what their color; equal in importance no matter what their texture."

Maya Angelou

It takes a variety of helpers to form a competent team. The best mixture includes recovering addicts, non-recovering addicts, mental health workers, social workers, psychiatrists, and medical doctors. We need a variety of backgrounds to address the complexity of struggling addicts, and it's important to not let our insecurity about the letters after someone's name cause us to feel our contribution doesn't matter. Our clients need all of our observations and wisdom, and every one of us brings a necessary piece of the puzzle.

_____

_____

_____

_____

_____

_____

_____

_____

_____

_____

_____

_____

_____

_____

_____

_____

"Let us not underestimate how hard it is to be compassionate. Compassion is hard because it requires the inner disposition to go with others to place where they are weak, vulnerable, lonely, and broken. But this is not our spontaneous response to suffering. What we desire most is to do away with suffering by fleeing from it or finding a quick cure for it."

Henri J.M. Nouwen

From time to time we encounter a client who presents a story that seems so complex, so traumatic, and is peppered with so many losses that we feel overwhelmed. Our instinct is to feel despair and struggle with treatment planning that cannot possibly address the extent of their need in 30-45 days. We can create a meaningful short term and long term plan that realistically takes into account their situation. We can break it into pieces creating space for a doable plan.

_____

_____

_____

_____

_____

_____

_____

_____

_____

_____

_____

_____

_____

"The first lesson to learn is to resign oneself to the little difficulties in life, not to hit out at everything one comes up against. If one were able to manage this one would not need to cultivate great power; even one's presence would be healing."

Hazrat Inayat Khan

It really is the little things in our daily life that create stress. We can manage the big issues, such as serious illness, but not being able to find a parking spot at the mall can make us insane! Every day we're faced with broken equipment, fender-benders, lost crowns in the middle of an important presentation, losing our keys, or not having enough cash at the cash-only yogurt shop. None of these things change our lives, but the accumulation of them can shake us. Perspective is key, as well as a sense of humor. Stop being surprised when inconvenience happens. Oh, and it's not personal.

"Many people are like garbage trucks. They run around full of garbage, full of frustration, full of anger, and full of disappointment. As their garbage piles up, they look for a place to dump it. And if you let them, they'll dump it on you. So when someone wants to dump on you, don't take it personally. Just smile, wave, wish them well, and move on. Believe me. You'll be happier."

David J. Pollay, The Law of the Garbage Truck: How to Respond to People Who Dump on You, and How to Stop Dumping on Others

Our clients are full of pain and regret and it's not uncommon for them to direct their anger and fear toward the counselors who have made themselves available for support. It's not personal, yet it can still deplete our energy and be discouraging. Then again, a while later we will hear from this same troubling client who has put together a year of recovery and is calling to thank us. Treasure these times.

_____

_____

_____

_____

_____

_____

_____

_____

_____

_____

_____

_____

"I believe the world is divided in three groups: givers, takers and the few that can balance both impulses. Giving and loving is a beautiful thing. It is the currency of compassion and kindness, it is what separates good people from the rest. And without it, the world would be a bleak place. If you are a giver, it is wise to define your boundaries because takers will take what you allow them to; all givers must learn to protect that about themselves or eventually, there is nothing left to give."

Tiffany Madison

Many helpers are more comfortable with giving than receiving. In fact, we may become uncomfortable when someone wants to offer us kindness or offers to assist us. We are so worried about being a burden or looking "needy." Receiving allows others to have the joy of giving, it truly is an exchange and creates mutuality and balance in the relationship.

_____

_____

_____

_____

_____

_____

_____

_____

_____

_____

_____

_____

_____

_____

_____

"Before you can live a part of you has to die. You have to let go of what could have been, how you should have acted and what you wish you would have said differently. You have to accept that you can't change the past experiences, opinions of others at that moment in time or outcomes from their choices or yours. When you finally recognize that truth then you will understand the true meaning of forgiveness of yourself and others. From this point you will finally be free."

Shannon L. Alder

Regrets can weigh heavy on recovering clients, and counselors often have their own unresolved regrets. We have areas where despite our step work we may not have truly forgiven ourselves, and may be over-giving and over-doing to somehow "make-up" for what it is we regret. It's impossible to truly forgive others when we have not experienced the freedom of forgiveness ourselves.

_____

_____

_____

_____

_____

_____

_____

_____

_____

_____

_____

_____

February 13 — Cynicism

"When emotions turn and stay sour, when thoughts become cynical and judgmental, good and compassionate treatment is on the line. Helpers who become sour and cynical tend to begrudge their high need clients for their neediness. There is a risk that helpers become too well-practiced at taking a bleak view of those they have avowed to assist. There is a temptation to begin to blame clients for their failure to improve. If treatment ends pre-maturely, with either a client never returning to treatment or a helper 'firing' them out of frustration, there is a tendency for the client to take the fall. Of course what we are talking about here are signs of burnout."

Scott E. Spradlin

It's hard to be lied to so often, and have our willingness to be of service interpreted as weakness. When we're running ourselves ragged and client service begins to feel like an imposition, we may avoid our clients as "takers." Self-care is NOT optional for caregivers.

_____

_____

_____

_____

_____

_____

_____

_____

_____

_____

_____

"Don't forget to pause and nourish yourself a bit along the way. When you're born to help others sometimes you forget to help yourself."

Paula Heller Garland

My friend calls this "Singles Awareness Day" because there is so much emphasis on romance. I have sat with tearful clients for 25 years, disappointed even IN relationships because they are not acknowledged. We need to be the love of our own lives, and today is a good day to celebrate your relationship with you. It's a time to remember that you aren't alone when you're in your own company. If you want flowers, order yourself a big fat bouquet! If you want chocolates, run down to See's. You are your Valentine.

_____

_____

_____

_____

_____

_____

_____

_____

_____

_____

_____

_____

_____

_____

_____

_____

_____

February 15 — Image Management

"Like a Columbus of the heart, mind and soul I have hurled myself off the shores of my own fears and limiting beliefs to venture far out into the uncharted territories of my inner truth, in search of what it means to be genuine and at peace with who I really am. I have abandoned the masquerade of living up to the expectations of others and explored the new horizons of what it means to be truly and completely me, in all my amazing imperfection and most splendid insecurity."

Anthon St. Maarten

How much are you still controlled by the image you maintain? Maybe it's an image that gets a lot of approval, and creates security for you. But how secure is it really? How obligated are you to the self you've constructed? Perhaps there are other layers of you to explore; are you ever curious?

FEBRUARY 16 — RECEIVING

"I don't see myself very clearly.

Then look at the people who love you...Look into their eyes and see what they're seeing; that's all you need to know yourself."

Armistead Maupin, The Night Listener

We all have area of blindness and self-deception. We have old wounds, so old that we believe they are our nature rather than defenses. And some of us don't give ourselves much grace. We need to have ourselves mirrored back to us by people who love us, who see our value, who don't judge our quirks but find them endearing. This is the view God has of us, reflected in the eyes of the people who love you.

_____

_____

_____

_____

_____

_____

_____

_____

_____

_____

_____

_____

_____

_____

_____

_____

_____

"Security is mostly a superstition. It does not exist in nature, nor do the children of men as a whole experience it. Avoiding danger is no safer in the long run than outright exposure. Life is either a daring adventure or nothing. "

Helen Keller

How much do you build adventure into your daily life? Do you try new things, new routes, new foods, or new challenges? Sometimes we're so afraid of looking stupid or being vulnerable that we refuse new opportunities just to be safe. Over time we begin to dry up, get more rigid, more inflexible. We need to regain our sense of humor to have the perspective to not take ourselves overly seriously. Remember that laughter at ourselves opens the door to shared experience.

_____

_____

_____

_____

_____

_____

_____

_____

_____

_____

_____

_____

_____

_____

_____

_____

"Talking to a therapist, I thought, was like taking your clothes off and then taking your skin off, and then having the other person say, "Would you mind opening up your rib cage so that we can start?"

Julie Schumacher, Black Box

The intimacy of the counseling relationship can open us in places we never expected or even knew were there. This is why the therapeutic alliance requires so much trust. Addicts and alcoholics are so shame based, and holding them in warm regard regardless of where the conversation leads them, is a profound gift to them. It's a shared gift, because there's nothing they're going to say that we are not capable of ourselves. It's a shared journey, which makes it so precious.

_____
_____
_____
_____
_____
_____
_____
_____
_____
_____
_____
_____
_____
_____
_____

FEBRUARY 19 — SELF-FORGIVENESS

"Life is too short to waste any amount of time on wondering what other people think about you. In the first place, if they had better things going on in their lives, they wouldn't have the time to sit around and talk about you. What's important to me is not others' opinions of me, but what's important to me is my opinion of myself."

C. JoyBell C.

In recovery we often say that, "What other people say about you is none of your business." We care so much about the way we're seen and can be sensitive when we remember our old behavior, and the pain we caused others in our addiction. When we look in the mirror we need to see ourselves accurately - see the changes we've made in our lives and see the living amends we make on a daily basis. This reduces our shame, and allows us to disconnect from the image we fight to protect.

_____

_____

_____

_____

_____

_____

_____

_____

_____

_____

_____

_____

_____

"If we can give up attachment to our roles as helpers, then maybe our clients can give up attachment to their roles as patients and we can meet as fellow souls on this incredible journey. We can fulfill the duties of our roles without being trapped by over-identification with them."

Ram Dass

We work in treatment as a fellow traveler. Many of us have walked the same path, for similar reasons, and are tempted to hide behind our role as "staff" and pretend to ourselves and others that we've moved beyond that time in our lives. The remnants of that life are etched in who we are, and this is something we can treasure about us rather than pretend no longer exists. This shared history gives us a unique understanding of those we serve, and can be a well of much needed patience.

_____
_____
_____
_____
_____
_____
_____
_____
_____
_____
_____
_____
_____
_____

FEBRUARY 21 — SELF-ACCEPTANCE

"Monsters were wild. Monsters were strong. Monsters were fierce and free. If I was monstrous...perhaps it wasn't such a bad thing."

Sarah Diemer

Helpers are often uncomfortable with conflict and while we believe anger is healing, in theory, we certainly don't want to experience it ourselves! Maybe we grew up with violence and avoid all shades of anger seeing it as inevitably turning into destructive rage. We all have a monstrous, heartless, raging side that is designed to protect us and address injustice in our lives. There are times when we need to access the parts of us that scare us and channel this part in to self-care and self-respect. When you acknowledge who you are you have choices.

"Take a step back. Draw in a deep breath. Now ask your-self, 'So what?' Then, after answering, ask yourself again, 'So what?' And then a third time—'So what?' Chances are you'll come to realize that the issue at hand is not as dire, detrimental, or important as you first thought."

Richelle E. Goodrich, Smile Anyway: Quotes, Verse, & Grumblings for Every Day of the Year

In Cognitive Behavioral Therapy there is a downward arrow technique that allows us to drill down to our core beliefs. Common ones include, "I am not love-able," and "I don't matter." We may have chosen to enter the counseling field in an attempt to matter, and this will lead to disappointment when clients relapse. Our work cannot provide value to us that we don't already have. Work is an expression of our value not our definition.

"Do not be afraid to color outside the lines. Take risks and do not be afraid to fail. Know that when the world knocks you down, the best revenge is to get up and continue forging ahead. Do not be afraid to be different or to stand up for what's right. Never quiet your voice to make someone else feel comfortable. No one remembers the person that fits in. It's the one who stands out that people will not be able to forget."

Nancy Arroyo Ruffin,
Letters to My Daughter: A Collection of Short Stories and Poems about Love, Pride, and Identity

When I read this I thought about running with scissors for some reason, and recognize how many of us feel like we never got the "manual" that everyone else seemed to get. We made up our lives as we went along! As a result, we can give ourselves permission to embrace our off-center selves, knowing that our clients will resonate with us.

FEBRUARY 24 — COGNITIVE FLEXIBILITY

"The very nature of the world is constant change. You set a goal and create a plan to achieve it; then the assumptions on which you based your plan change - they always do. The challenge is to retain your goals while adapting your tactics. Relax and stay flexible in order to reach your goals and maintain your happiness.

Jonathan Lockwood Huie

Recovery includes a shift in our black-and-white thinking. This can make life more grey, open up more competing priorities, and make situations multi-dimensional. Life becomes more complicated, and we are required to be more flexible. Cognitive flexibility is a hallmark of intellectual and emotional security, and our work with clients includes modeling this for them as they heal their underused frontal lobe. We are able to spot options and problem solve in ways they can't until they have more sobriety. It helps if we're doing this in our own recovery!

"You are not broken. You are not a problem to be solved. Solving your "problem", whatever you perceive your problem or problems to be, is not the key to happiness."

Golda Poretsky

Members of the Twelve Step culture frequently identify as "addicts" and "alcoholics" at the meeting level. There are those that believe that identifying with our disease labels us as "ill," instead of seeing us as whole people. My experience is that identifying as addicts and alcoholics combats our impressive ability to "forget" our addiction. Remembering our disease prompts us to act on our own behalf and pay attention to our mind, body, and spirit to keep the health and lives we have worked so hard to obtain.

_____

_____

_____

_____

_____

_____

_____

_____

_____

_____

_____

_____

_____

_____

_____

_____

Two Wolves

One evening an old Cherokee told his grandson about a battle that goes on inside people. He said, "My son, the battle is between two 'wolves' inside us all.

One is Evil. It is anger, envy, jealousy, sorrow, regret, greed, arrogance, self-pity, guilt, resentment, Inferiority, lies, false pride, superiority and ego.

The other is Good. It is joy, peace, love, hope, serenity, humility, kindness, benevolence, empathy, generosity, truth, compassion and faith."

The grandson thought about it for a minute and then asked his grandfather, "Which wolf wins?" The old Cherokee simply replied, "The one you feed."

_____

_____

_____

_____

_____

_____

_____

_____

_____

_____

_____

_____

_____

_____

_____

_____

_____

_____

_____

"Gratitude unlocks the fullness of life. It turns what we have into enough, and more. It can turn a meal into a feast, a house into a home, a stranger into a friend. It turns denial into acceptance, chaos to order, confusion to clarity. It turns problems into gifts, failures into success, the unexpected into perfect timing, and mistakes into important events. Gratitude makes sense of our past, brings peace for today and creates a vision for tomorrow."

Melody Beattie

Many of us are familiar with the classic sponsor assignment to write a gratitude list every day for two weeks. It's designed to help us turn our attention to small kindnesses and unexpected delights that present themselves. Annoyances and challenges show up as frequently as happy surprises - we can remember that we can choose our focus.

_____

_____

_____

_____

_____

_____

_____

_____

_____

_____

_____

_____

_____

"When enforcing our boundaries, first and foremost, we are caring for ourselves, but we are also helping others to have a clear understanding of what we consider acceptable behavior. We are reflecting back to them what is not acceptable and, therefore, providing them an opportunity to consider that information and make necessary changes."

Donna Wood

Our clients often struggle with social skills and are frequently unaware of how much space to take up, how loud they are, how to use humor appropriately... they can be intrusive as they bounce their way around the treatment center. This includes the way clients interact with us, and we need to be willing to give them feedback we would normally avoid in a social situation. It's unkind to notice socially awkward behavior and not give clients the opportunity to change it.

"The world gives us PLENTY of opportunities to strengthen our patience. While this truth can definitely be challenging, this is a good thing. Patience is a key that unlocks the door to a more fulfilling life. It is through a cultivation of patience that we become better parents, powerful teachers, great businessmen, good friends, and a live a happier life."

Steve Maraboli, Life, the Truth, and Being Free

Some people are easier to be patient with than others. Perhaps we have a lazy coworker, a critical supervisor, or a client that challenges our authority. It takes extra energy to be patient with people who are prickly or passive aggressive, and we can get resentful towards them. Perhaps we can imagine that they present us with an emotional gymnasium where we can develop new patience muscles.

_____
_____
_____
_____
_____
_____
_____
_____
_____
_____
_____
_____
_____
_____

MARCH 1 — SELF-ACCEPTANCE

"One of the best guides to how to be self-loving is to give ourselves the love we are often dreaming about receiving from others. There was a time when I felt lousy about my over-forty body, saw myself as too fat, too this, or too that. Yet I fantasized about finding a lover who would give me the gift of being loved as I am. It is silly, isn't it, that I would dream of someone else offering to me the acceptance and affirmation I was withholding from myself. This was a moment when the maxim "You can never love anybody if you are unable to love yourself" made clear sense. And I add, "Do not expect to receive the love from someone else you do not give yourself."

Bell Hooks, All About Love: New Visions

Many of us spend years looking outside of ourselves hoping to feel completed and valuable. We dream of feeling loveable and it never occurs to us that we can love ourselves. Maybe it's time to make a date night with yourself!

_____

_____

_____

_____

_____

_____

_____

_____

_____

_____

_____

"Understanding the difference between healthy striving and perfectionism is critical to laying down the shield and picking up your life. Research shows that perfectionism hampers success. In fact, it's often the path to depression, anxiety, addiction, and life paralysis."

Brené Brown, The Gifts of Imperfection:
Let Go of Who You Think You're Supposed to Be and
Embrace Who You Are

Some of us believe that perfection is possible, and become paralyzed in our attempts to meet those standards. Perfection's a moving target, always just out of our grasp while giving us just enough hope to keep us trying. It's like a really bad relationship! It has the same outcome as a relationship with someone unavailable -we get tied up in knots and our personality deteriorates.

_____

_____

_____

_____

_____

_____

_____

_____

_____

_____

_____

_____

_____

_____

March 3 — Ego

"Make your ego porous. Will is of little importance, complaining is nothing, fame is nothing. Openness, patience, receptivity, solitude is everything."

Rainer Maria Rilke

I know all too well how much this is easier said than done. While I have a fantasy picture of myself as being open and flexible, I am reminded from time that this is just an illusion! It is impossible to be self-defensive and receptive simultaneously. Perhaps it's wiser to admit our ego wound and step away for a short time to gather ourselves and become receptive again. I know when I'm in this place when I'm thinking about my rebuttal as the person is speaking. This is a terrible listening habit! This can be particularly troubling for addiction counselors because the stakes are so high. The mortality from drug and alcohol use is high, so the desire to convince is always tempting.

_____

_____

_____

_____

_____

_____

_____

_____

_____

_____

_____

_____

_____

"Water does not resist. Water flows. When you plunge your hand into it, all you feel is a caress. Water is not a solid wall, it will not stop you. But water always goes where it wants to go, and nothing in the end can stand against it. Water is patient. Dripping water wears away a stone. Remember that, my child. Remember you are half water. If you can't go through an obstacle, go around it. Water does".

Margaret Atwood, The Penelopiad

Eastern faiths use this analogy often, particularly Taoism. It's a powerful image, because water is both soft and corrosive. Martial arts frequently refers to moving with and not against energy. Even small movements applied persistently are powerful and convincing. Your steady, loving presence with your clients has the same effect as they are gently moved by your persistent, reliable presence.

_____

_____

_____

_____

_____

_____

_____

_____

_____

_____

_____

_____

_____

March 5 — The fairness police

"It can be deeply frustrating when people disagree with you, especially when it is so many of them. It might make you feel slighted, or even isolated. But instead of declaring everyone to be stupid, and looking for ways to reinforce your position, try learning WHY they disagree. It might be surprising and refreshing to learn that you're not alone in a world of stupid people. Just people with divergent philosophies and life experiences; different sets of priorities. It's much more rewarding than being continually outraged and alone in your own head, forever declaring yourself to be the only one who cares, the only one smart enough to think like you think. Give yourself a break from your solitary supremacy. You might sleep easier."

Orsov

Some of us are easily prone to offense; we walk around in the world with our fairness police ticket pad and feel a compulsion to correct the behaviors and thoughts of others. Is this you?

_____

_____

_____

_____

_____

_____

_____

_____

_____

_____

_____

_____

March 6 — Detachment

"I'm inclined to reserve all judgments, a habit that has opened up many curious natures to me and also made me the victim of not a few veteran bores."

F. Scott Fitzgerald, The Great Gatsby

I found this quote hilarious because it's true that an attitude of openness is not discriminating, and we can be taken hostage by people with enormous amounts of need simply because we displayed courtesy and interest. Being a compassionate person does not require us to suffer hours in the company of people who offer us little in exchange, and we are not obligated to like people simply because they like us. It's possible to treat people kindly without allowing energy vampires to suck us dry. This is the value of detachment. I can observe your behavior, not judge it, and not participate in it.

_____

_____

_____

_____

_____

_____

_____

_____

_____

_____

_____

_____

_____

_____

My fear of being real, of being seen, paralyzes me into silence. I crave the touch and the connection, but I'm not always brave enough to open my hand and reach out. This is the great challenge: to be seen, accepted, and loved, I must first reveal, offer, and surrender."

> Anna White, Mended: Thoughts on Life, Love,
> and Leaps of Faith

Many of us were deprived of accurate response and understanding as children, and don't trust even the honest attempts of others to connect with us, too frightened of the potential rejection to initiate contact. So we are lonely, and keep waiting for other people to assure us they're safe, PROVE that they're safe. What if we went first to just jump in the pool and issued that invitation to coffee? What if?

March 8 — Resilience

"There's a drive in a lost soul—in one that is searching for acceptance, companionship, belonging, whatever you want to call it. The slightest coincidence ignites a spark that one hopes will lead to something meaningful."

Doug Cooper, Outside In

Our clients have so much more resilience than they recognize. They are survivors of trauma, survivors of discrimination and abandonment, and still they arrive at our center bedraggled but alive. Many people never make it to us, so those that do have a spark somewhere, a light that has pulled them to shore. We get to remind them of this and help them find and develop the strengths that have made them who they are, even with scar tissue. Don't mistake being sucked-up with weakness. They often have spines of steel. You did, didn't you when you first got clean?

_____

_____

_____

_____

_____

_____

_____

_____

_____

_____

_____

_____

_____

March 9 — Footwork

"Patience is a virtue, but there comes a moment when you must stop being patient and take the day by the throat and shake it. If it fights back; fine. I'd rather end up bloody at the end of the day, then unhurt with no progress made, no knowledge gained. I'd rather have a no, then nothing. I'd forgotten that about myself."

Laurell K. Hamilton

This is the footwork part of the program, the time when we have to GO to the interview, challenge the bully, leave the toxic friendship, give life a shot. We can surrender the outcome, but we need to move forward and be willing to scrape our knee and keep walking. Our clients did this to maintain their addiction every day, so they have it in them. It's matter of channeling this energy toward their best interests instead of self-destruction.

_____

_____

_____

_____

_____

_____

_____

_____

_____

_____

_____

_____

_____

_____

MARCH 10 — UNFINISHED BUSINESS

"Karma does never return to punish. Its role is to assist with solving what has been left uncompleted. It always returns to you, when you are strong enough to look at it. You never are asked to deal with more than you can handle. So relax and accept what is being offered to you. Accept it as a gift of love."

Raphael Zernoff

Many of us have years of patterns. We have the insanity of dating the same person in a new outfit over and over again. We choose unwise work situations despite the obvious red flags over and over again. What's left unfinished that we keep returning to the same conflicts, the same dilemmas? There's a story here, a message and lesson in these choices rather than simply the stupidity we label them to be. We're presented with opportunities to heal these open wounds everyday if we recognize them for what they are.

"And second, everyone is so weird, but they're all completely accepted. It's like, okay, you have a pumpkin head, and that guy's made of tin, and you're a talking chicken, but what the hell, let's do a road trip."

Rebecca Makkai, The Borrower

My favorite part about recovery is the cast of characters that fill the meetings. There's room for everyone — the guy that talks to himself, the woman who drinks 7 cups of coffee, the guy that laughs too loud, the sad woman in the corner who sits and cries and never speaks. The age range, from elderly to young, and the diversity of cultures all make a wonderful stew. No matter where you attend a meeting in the world you will experience this sense that everyone in the room is SUPPOSED to be in the room, and that means you.

_____
_____
_____
_____
_____
_____
_____
_____
_____
_____
_____
_____
_____
_____

"Compassion hurts. When you feel connected to every-thing, you also feel responsible for everything. And you cannot turn away. Your destiny is bound with the destinies of others. You must either learn to carry the Universe or be crushed by it. You must grow strong enough to love the world, yet empty enough to sit down at the same table with its worst horrors."

Andrew Boyd, Daily Afflictions: The Agony of Being
Connected to Everything in the Universe

An ethical principle for chemical dependency counselors is to acknowledge the responsibility of our work with others. We impact people's lives at a time when they are most vulnerable, and we need to be comfortable with this responsibility without being overwhelmed by it. This means we need to hold ourselves accountable to our ethical codes and take time to shore ourselves up to avoid burn-out.

March 13 — Taking a risk

"The four stages of acceptance:
1. This is worthless nonsense.
2. This is an interesting, but perverse, point of view.
3. This is true, but quite unimportant.
4. I always said so."

J.B.S. Haldane

Have you ever known someone who has to make any idea HIS idea before it's a valid one? Are you one of those people? Many of us have a pessimistic protective mechanism that compels us to say "no" first, to everything, and then allow ourselves to be talked into things. This is hard on people around us; coming up against the "no" person is too hard, so they are often excluded from conversations. The push back is too much effort and creates discouragement for others. To change this you must come to terms with the possibility of mistakes, or being foolish, and believe you can get over it. I promise that you will and you'll probably have more friends.

"For the wise have always known that no one can make much of his life until self-searching has become a regular habit, until he is able to admit and accept what he finds, and until he patiently and persistently tries to correct what is wrong."

Bill Wilson

I was struck with the "admit and accept what he finds" in this passage, because that really is the heart of the matter, isn't it? We don't want to open that closet and discover something about us that we believe we can't live with. There may be something so monstrous and unlovable about us that exposing it would eliminate all possible affection from others. This is why sponsors are so helpful. They can listen to the worst of our lives, the foolish and deadly mistakes we've made, and turn to us to say, "Is that all you have?" demonstrating that there's nothing we can say that makes us less than human. What a relief!

_____

_____

_____

_____

_____

_____

_____

_____

_____

_____

_____

_____

MARCH 15 — RADICAL SELF-CARE

"Radical self-care is what we've been longing for, desperate for, our entire lives--friendship with our own hearts."

Anne Lamott

What would radical self-care mean to you?

Maybe saying no to a loved one who is a professional "guilter" and not be guilty. Maybe giving someone some money to get a cab to the airport instead of dragging yourself out at 3:00 am? Maybe taking a nap in the middle of the day or not working on Christmas even though you don't have children and will be at home with your cats and everyone else has children? How supremely selfish are you willing to be in your own recovery? It means taking care of ourselves the way we would take care of our best friend, someone we love and who is dear to us. This is the art of reparenting because we didn't get the nurturing we needed when we needed it. It's not too late!

_____

_____

_____

_____

_____

_____

_____

_____

_____

_____

_____

"You have a great body. It is an intricate piece of technology and a sophisticated super-computer. It runs on peanuts and even regenerates itself. Your relationship with your body is one of the most important relationships you'll ever have. And since repairs are expensive and spare parts are hard to come by, it pays to make that relationship good."

Steve Goodier

There's a lot of research demonstrating the corrosive effects of stress on the human body. Our adrenal glands become fatigued, and we can't respond well to the events around us. Our bodies are precious and they need to last for the rest of our lives. While science has developed prosthesis, they are not a goal! Put in the effort to keep your own teeth, strengthen your own bones and hips, and breathe your own air. Sure you can get new hips or an oxygen tank, but you can also keep your own.

"When it comes to the crusty behavior of some people, give them the benefit of the doubt. They may be drowning right before your eyes, but you can't see it. And you'd never ask someone to drown with a smile on his face."

Richelle E. Goodrich, Smile Anyway: Quotes, Verse, & Grumblings for Every Day of the Year

The human response to anxiety is to avoid the source of anxiety – to look away from that which frightens us and causes us discomfort. You may have noticed this when you avoid eye contact with a client in group or a co-worker in a staff meeting. Eye contact invites conversation and we are side-stepping this possibility. Recognizing your avoidant behavior is the start to healing what scares you. Most likely there's something in that person that would make you very uncomfortable if it were true about you. Maybe it's your "inner blowhard" or "inner whiner" you're really avoiding!

_____

_____

_____

_____

_____

_____

_____

_____

_____

_____

_____

_____

_____

"People say that what we're all seeking is a meaning for life. I don't think that's what we're really seeking. I think that what we're seeking is an experience of being alive, so that our life experiences on the purely physical plane will have resonances within our innermost being and reality, so that we actually feel the rapture of being alive."

Joseph Campbell

How alive do you feel at work? Do you find ways to energize yourself and celebrate victories with clients, no matter how small? There's energy to draw from and mystery to tap into that creates a sense of wonder in what we do. Sometimes the most amazing thing will come out of our moth during a session, and we KNOW it didn't come from us. We are channels for this mystery if we let ourselves be. Opening ourselves up to this possibility gives us an incredible amount of curiosity about what each day will bring.

_____

_____

_____

_____

_____

_____

_____

_____

_____

_____

_____

_____

_____

_____

"People will always notice something about you. It might be the way you walk or the way you talk, or just simply your personality. Live each day in the way you want to be remembered. Live in such a way that people will be inspired by those unique qualities that you have and strive to live better lives for themselves."

Amaka Imani Nkosazana

We influence others in so many different ways. 70% of communication is non-verbal so it's our tone of voice, body language, facial expressions, and emotional and physical availability that communicates who we are to those around us. Simple kindnesses like a brief touch on the shoulder of support, or a smile during group can make an enormous impact on someone and will be remembered far longer than the situation itself. Native Americans ask, "What kind of ancestor do you want to be?"

_____

_____

_____

_____

_____

_____

_____

_____

_____

_____

_____

_____

_____

"The woman gestured to a seat and put on a patient face. An impatient sort of patient face, like an impatient face dressing up as a patient one for Halloween."

Shannon Hale, Midnight in Austenland

This quote made me smile because I have been this woman, and figured I was fooling people with my patient face! The end of the shift is a tough time for staff. We've responded to crisis, played phone tag with probation officers, led groups, filled out paperwork, and our ears are tired from listening. Then a client pops in, filled with fear, and we know this may take a while. We sit down, take a deep breath, and focus. This is professional in us, the part that keeps our irritation in check and remembers we're there to serve.

_____

_____

_____

_____

_____

_____

_____

_____

_____

_____

_____

_____

_____

_____

_____

_____

"Anyway, I keep picturing all these little kids playing some game in this big field of rye and all. Thousands of little kids, and nobody's around - nobody big, I mean - except me. And I'm standing on the edge of some crazy cliff. What I have to do, I have to catch everybody if they start to go over the cliff - I mean if they're running and they don't look where they're going I have to come out from somewhere and catch them. That's all I do all day. I'd just be the catcher in the rye and all. I know it's crazy, but that's the only thing I'd really like to be."

J.D. Salinger, The Catcher in the Rye

Sometimes it can feel like we're running around putting out fires all day. There are certainly times when we feel like we're the only "big person" in the room, as clients act out all around us. Much like the catcher above, we frequently say "play the tape all the way through," or help them break situations into manageable pieces, and it's what WE love to do!

_____

_____

_____

_____

_____

_____

_____

_____

_____

_____

_____

_____

March 22 — Scar tissue

"This is how the soul heals. It thaws out bit by bit, the way the ground warms after a hard winter. You notice the sun or hear the whippoorwill calling across the flats. You sweep your porch, go drink coffee in the shade of the trumpet vines. You have days where you want to lay down and die, but what you learn is this: As long as there's somebody left on this earth who loves you, it's reason enough to stay alive. You don't give in to your broke heart-- you just let the wide, cracked space fill up again."

Michael Lee West, American Pie

Addiction leaves wide cracks filled with scar tissue across our hearts. Some of our clients have burned bridges in the process, and there may not be a person who loves them. It may be the counseling staff who stands in as part of the recovering community and extends the love of the fellowship to the client. We may offer the first experience of acceptance and belonging they have felt in a very long time.

MARCH 23 — SHATTERING ILLUSIONS

"With me, illusions are bound to be shattered. I am here to shatter all illusions. Yes, it will irritate you, it will annoy you - that's my way of functioning and working. I will sabotage you from your very roots! Unless you are totally destroyed as a mind, there is no hope for you."

Osho

What a great description of what we do for a living! We shatter client illusions about the role of drugs and alcohol in their lives; we annoy them by challenging their patterns of thinking and self-sabotage belief systems. We catch them in the middle of relapse set-ups and offer them healthy alternatives. Recovery requires us to pull up old thinking by the roots, and replant new ones. So, I guess that means we're farmers!

_____

_____

_____

_____

_____

_____

_____

_____

_____

_____

_____

_____

_____

_____

_____

_____

"Usually, when the distractions of daily life deplete our energy, the first thing we eliminate is the thing we need the most: quiet, reflective time. Time to dream, time to contemplate what's working and what's not, so that we can make changes for the better. (January 17)"

Sarah Ban Breathnach

How true this is for so many of us. We tell ourselves we don't have time to rest, to take a vacation, or hang out with a friend. We'll do it when things "settle down." It's easy to become disconnected from ourselves, putting our fingers in the dyke to keep the damn from bursting and our inner chaos becoming obvious to everyone. Our longevity in the addiction field depends on our self-care. We can't give what we don't have.

_____

_____

_____

_____

_____

_____

_____

_____

_____

_____

_____

_____

_____

_____

_____

MARCH 25 — CONNECTING

"I believe that you control your destiny, that you can be what you want to be. You can also stop and say, 'No, I won't do it, I won't behave his way anymore. I'm lonely and I need people around me, maybe I have to change my methods of behaving,' and then you do it."

Leo Buscaglia

Addiction is ultimately profoundly lonely. It's impossible to have an intimate relationship with others when we are so absent from ourselves! We have the opportunity to meet people in this isolated place and reach in because they may have forgotten how to reach out. We can role model authenticity and congruence in our interactions with them and invite them into a healthy relationship with us.

_____

_____

_____

_____

_____

_____

_____

_____

_____

_____

_____

_____

_____

_____

_____

_____

_____

March 26 — Complaining

"See if you can catch yourself complaining, in either speech or thought, about a situation you find yourself in, what other people do or say, your surroundings, your life situation, even the weather. To complain is always nonacceptance of what is. It invariably carries an unconscious negative charge. When you complain, you make yourself into a victim. When you speak out, you are in your power. So change the situation by taking action or by speaking out if necessary or possible; leave the situation or accept it. All else is madness."

Eckhart Tolle

Did you ever notice that some people bond with each other by complaining? They create a negative bond between them and it becomes the center of the relationship. Some of us work in facilities where this negative bond is normal. However, tactfully excusing yourself when negative conversation is going on will create a signal for others who are also tired of the negativity and they'll find you! It's worth a try.

_____

_____

_____

_____

_____

_____

_____

_____

_____

_____

MARCH 27 — IMPERFECTION

"We're all fools," said Clemens, "all the time. It's just we're a different kind each day. We think, I'm not a fool today. I've learned my lesson. I was a fool yesterday but not this morning. Then tomorrow we find out that, yes, we were a fool today too. I think the only way we can grow and get on in this world is to accept the fact we're not perfect and live accordingly."

Ray Bradbury, The Illustrated Man

Any time we learn something new we have a learning curve, which means we might look awkward or even silly. We'll make mistakes and have to ask for directions. Clients will lie to us and "get over," and we will have to apologize more than once to our co-workers over time. Serenity will require us to find peace with our imperfections and stop taking ourselves so seriously. A sense of humor about ourselves will save us on a regular basis.

_____

_____

_____

_____

_____

_____

_____

_____

_____

_____

_____

_____

_____

MARCH 28 — REGRETS

"The feelings that hurt most, the emotions that sting most, are those that are absurd - The longing for impossible things, precisely because they are impossible; nostalgia for what never was; the desire for what could have been; regret over not being someone else; dissatisfaction with the world's existence. All these half-tones of the soul's consciousness create in us a painful landscape, an eternal sunset of what we are."

Fernando Pessoa

Have you ever heard the phrase, "I miss the family I never had"? We may struggle with the "could haves" and "should haves," and regrets over opportunities we lost in our addition. It may be true that we will never be a prima ballerina or the CEO of Microsoft, but we have plenty of challenges and relationships ahead of us in recovery. Our early ambitions are still part of us, and it may be that they're possible in another form. Let your imagination guide you.

_____

_____

_____

_____

_____

_____

_____

_____

_____

_____

_____

_____

March 29 — Daily rituals

"It is all gone, thought Peter. All of it is gone! And there is no way to get it back.

'Eat,' said Leo Matienne again, very gently.

Peter looked the truth of what he had lost full in the face. And then he ate."

Kate DiCamillo, The Magician's Elephant

When the world falls out beneath our feet, and we're in a free-fall, the simple routines of life like eating, sleeping, and our daily coffee ritual can be enormously grounding and comforting. Rituals remind us that life is not over, that much of the world continues on, and eventually so will we. Asking clients to build in daily self-care rituals as part of their recovery will help sustain them when they are stressed or face disappointments. Remember this when you remind them to eat breakfast or do their morning meditation and they act like you're nagging. If they can build these habits now they will be part of their relapse prevention plan.

_____

_____

_____

_____

_____

_____

_____

_____

_____

_____

MARCH 30 — FIXING OTHERS

"Many times when we help we do not really serve. . . . Serving is also different from fixing. One of the pioneers of the Human Potential Movement, Abraham Maslow, said, "If all you have is a hammer, everything looks like a nail.' Seeing yourself as a fixer may cause you to see brokenness everywhere, to sit in judgment of life itself. When we fix others, we may not see their hidden wholeness or trust the integrity of the life in them. Fixers trust their own expertise. When we serve, we see the unborn wholeness in others; we collaborate with it and strengthen it. Others may then be able to see their wholeness for themselves for the first time."

Rachel Naomi Remen

Clients don't come to us as a blank slate – they have a wealth of strengths and experiences that we can help them discover. Fixing them, giving them the answers, cripples them and ultimately communicates disrespect for their individual recovery path.

_____

_____

_____

_____

_____

_____

_____

_____

_____

_____

_____

_____

March 31 — Priorities

"Here's a nice image for a life in balance," she said. "You're juggling these four balls that you've named work, family, friends, spirit. Now, work is a rubber ball. If you drop it, it bounces back. The other balls they're made of glass." "I've dropped a few of those glass balls in my day. Sometimes they chip, sometimes they shatter to pieces."

James Patterson, Roses are Red

Work bounces because it's always there. We go on vacation, and our clients and the paperwork are waiting for us when we get back. Being unavailable for our friends and family can result in a distance we may have to work very hard to repair. Are you allowing work to interfere in the relationships that matter most to you? Are you spending time with your Higher Power, or are you skipping meetings to finish paperwork? Spend some time with your priorities today.

_____

_____

_____

_____

_____

_____

_____

_____

_____

_____

_____

_____

April 1 — Blind spots

"The Soul Toupee is that thing about ourselves we are most deeply embarrassed by and like to think we have cunningly concealed from the world, but which is, in fact, pitifully obvious to everybody who knows us."

Tim Kreider, We Learn Nothing

I love the "Soul Toupee" image! These are the embarrassing parts of us that peak out when we east expect it, and wish we could deny or at least blame on someone else! I'm reminded of someone I met once who specialized in spiritual forms of therapy. However, she was often irritated by the behavior of others, and when she would say something harsh she would start to smile. It was as though the smile was supposed to soften the message. I've always wondered how aware SHE is of the barely concealed, non-spiritual judgment she carries about other people. Technically, these are called blind spots and we all have them. Hopefully someone we trust will lovingly point them out.

_____

_____

_____

_____

_____

_____

_____

_____

_____

_____

_____

_____

"It's not that I believe everything happens for a reason. It's just that... I just think that some things are meant to be broken. Imperfect. Chaotic. It's the universe's way of providing contrast, you know? There have to be a few holes in the road. It's how life is."

Sarah Dessen, The Truth About Forever

This reminds me of the Native American custom of leaving imperfection in works of art to acknowledge that only the Great Spirit is perfect. When clients are faced with the wreckage of their disease the enormity of their losses can be overwhelming; stability seems very far away. Every moment of peace in recovery our clients experience is valuable. Every success, no matter how small, needs to be seen and contrasted with the chaos of their life in active addiction. Our clients are rebuilding and need every sign of resilience they can find to have the courage to move forward.

_____

_____

_____

_____

_____

_____

_____

_____

_____

_____

_____

_____

April 3 — Boundaries

"Everything has boundaries. The same holds true with thought. You shouldn't fear boundaries, but you should not be afraid of destroying them. That's what is most important if you want to be free: respect for and exasperation with boundaries."

Haruki Murakami, Colorless Tsukuru Tazaki
and His Years of Pilgrimage.

Many of our clients have confusion between walls and boundaries. Many of us do, also. When we don't trust our ability to tell the good guys from the bad guys we protect ourselves by keeping everyone out, "just in case." In recovery we're able to reconnect with our intuition and our observation skills. Boundaries are vital to our health and well-being, but walls can begin to close in around us and our world gets very small. If you struggle with walls it's important to work on lowering them to make yourself fully present for your clients and your co-workers.

_____

_____

_____

_____

_____

_____

_____

_____

_____

_____

_____

_____

"Life is not out to get you, even though it feels that way sometimes. You are totally safe every step of the way (at least you have the option of seeing life that way if you want to). Life is about learning to walk the tightrope, find your balance, and trust God, life and yourself in the process. And you can do this, because there is really nothing to fear. When you get this concept it is going to change everything."

Kimberly Giles, Choosing Clarity: The Path to Fearlessness

This quote reminds us that we have a choice about the way we see the world, and we have a choice to believe that we have what we need and that all is well. Most of our fear is triggered by future-tripping or feeling overwhelmed by remorse for a past we can't control or correct. When we stay in today we usually have everything we need, and our serenity returns.

_____
_____
_____
_____
_____
_____
_____
_____
_____
_____
_____
_____
_____
_____

"Always trust your fellow man. And always cut the cards. Always trust God. And always build your house on high ground. Always love thy neighbor. And always pick a good neighborhood to live in."

> *Robert Fulghum, All I Really Need to Know*
> *I Learned in Kindergarten*

This is a fabulous reminder of the importance of footwork in the program! Spiritual growth is a result of a partnership between us and our Higher Power. In recovery our ability to problem-solve increases, and we develop more opportunities to participate in life. We bring more to the table in our sobriety, and yet we still don't control the outcome of our efforts. Our job is to offer our best and trust that the results, even if disappointing, will still be in our best interests! I know, easier said than done!

_____

_____

_____

_____

_____

_____

_____

_____

_____

_____

_____

_____

_____

_____

"One of the symptoms of an approaching nervous breakdown is the belief that one's work is terribly important."

Bertrand Russell, The Conquest of Happiness

We're addressing the emotional and physical damage as a result of addiction every day. It can take its toll on us, and it's easy to begin to see the world as a dark place. We deal with a chronic and lethal disease, and it's possible for our work and sense of self to become heavy. What "nervous breakdown" used to refer to is overwhelming depression or anxiety which can manifest as burnout in the treatment business. While our work is important and we're up against a serious disease life also presents us with joy and personal idiosyncrasies to balance it. We need to be alert for those balancing parts of life.

_____

_____

_____

_____

_____

_____

_____

_____

_____

_____

_____

_____

_____

_____

April 7 — Problem-solving

"A light on my car's dashboard came on, and instead of fixing the problem, I waited for the bulb to burn out. Crisis solved."

Jarod Kintz, Sleepwalking is restercise

This is a common problem solving approach in addiction. We can add to this; waiting for a miracle, denial, blaming and complaining, and creating a crisis! These approaches can be frustrating for helpers. Clients will fail to provide the information we need to create a case management plan and then spring a last minute court appearance or upcoming community service obligation on us. We can caught up in their anxiety and reactivity, and cosign unstable plans. Soon, we'll receive a frantic call asking for our help to help the client clean up the consequences. Our job is to remain calm in the face of their urgency, not letting their emergency become our emergency.

_____

_____

_____

_____

_____

_____

_____

_____

_____

_____

_____

_____

_____

"I have a theory that burnout is about resentment. And you beat it by knowing what it is you're giving up that makes you resentful."

Marissa Mayer

This is an interesting thought. Our work requires sacrifice on our part. We devoted the time and money it took to become educated. We prepared for and passed the state certifying exam. We went through the job application process. All of this took time from our personal relationships, took financial planning, and we were required to stay focused for long periods of time. What happens when we don't feel we're being paid fairly? What if we're given a disappointing shift, or our caseload is much larger than we anticipated? It's important to address our concerns and either change the situation or change our expectations or we will leave the field tired and embittered. We need you.

_____

_____

_____

_____

_____

_____

_____

_____

_____

_____

_____

_____

"Listen to Mr. Complacency long enough and he'll convince you that what you really, really need is a nap."

Alex and Brett Harris

We all have an inner committee, comprised of different parts of ourselves and our history. There's often an inner critic, and irresponsible child, a part of us that tells us "F***it" when times get hard. There can also be that part of us that feels like we've worked hard enough. We've got a lot of clean time and since we work in recovery all day we don't need meetings any more. . . sound familiar? Yes, we're working in recovery, but we're focused on *other people's* recovery! Complacency takes a lot of us out. We relax our vigilance, and compare ourselves to our newcomer clients which leads us to believe we're "cured." We're working too closely with the disease, the active disease, to set ourselves up like that. We need more support, not less!

"Feeling bad is not the problem. The problem is that we feel bad about feeling bad. Once you begin to let go of feeling bad about feeling bad,and start feeling better about feeling bad, then pretty soon you'll just feel better. And then you'll feel awesome."

Eric Micha'el Leventhal

We can be so judgmental of our own thoughts. We assume that with solid recovery we should be more "spiritual," "patient," and have better self-esteem. The truth is we have these traits much more often than we did before, and yet they aren't going to be present 100% of the time. We're going to say stupid things, drop the ball, and get irritable with clients and coworkers sometimes. We're human, and we forget to apply the "Progress not Perfection" slogan that we use with our clients. We need to apply the same compassion towards ourselves that we extend to others.

April 11 — Healing

"Since I was young, I have always known this: Life damages us, every one. We can't escape that damage. But now, I am also learning this: We can be mended. We mend each other"

Veronica Roth

One of the benefits of helping is the opportunity to be in the presence of people who have amazing amounts of resilience. There are times when I've been spun out about something in my life, and as I'm listening to a client who's walking through something incredibly hard with dignity and grace, I'm given the gift of perspective. I'm able to follow her/his lead, unbeknownst to them. The truth is we're healed when we heal others. You can see this as the clients interact, and as they offer support and encouragement to each other. Recovery truly is about connection.

_____

_____

_____

_____

_____

_____

_____

_____

_____

_____

_____

_____

_____

_____

"But if you're gonna dine with them cannibals
Sooner or later, darling, you're gonna get eaten . . ."

Nick Cave

Recovering people are pretty risk adverse in interesting ways. We're willing to risk being eaten by cannibals, but we're not willing to go to that interview, or ask someone out to the movies. It can be confusing to family members who expect the same "courage" in recovery they thought the client was showing in their addiction. We may have seen this confusion in our own recovery, and were startled at how avoidant we could be. We may have judged ourselves pretty harshly, and may have even relapsed over this "weakness." Some of us didn't have a secure home base as a child, which would have given us the courage to explore the world. A sponsor or you, their counselor, could be that person for a client when they have never experienced this before. What a privilege!

_____
_____
_____
_____
_____
_____
_____
_____
_____
_____
_____
_____
_____

"There's that horrible-beautiful moment, that bitter-sweet impasse where you know that somebody is bullshitting you but they're doing it with such panache and conviction...no, it's because they say exactly what you want to hear, at that point in time."

Irvine Welsh, Porno

Don't we all crave a "co-signer" for our bullshit every now and then? In fact, most of us were pretty gifted at finding people like that in our addiction. While it's tempting to seek input from people who will agree with our version of reality – especially our version of ourselves as victims, it's the worst thing for us. We got clean and stayed clean because people were willing to be honest with us. As a counselor we are frequently in a position where we have to deliver painful or unwelcome feedback because we respect our clients enough to give the information they need to make REAL changes.

_____

_____

_____

_____

_____

_____

_____

_____

_____

_____

_____

_____

"When you are convinced that what you offer is yours, whether it be mediocre or of standard quality, your originality will make people love you in a way you did not expect."

Michael Bassey Johnson

As Interns, we were exposed to a variety of styles and some counselor approaches were more comfortable for us than others. This was especially true in psychoeducation. The group facilitation role is often difficult for counselors who are more comfortable in on–on-ones. Sometimes it feels like we aren't reaching the clients, maybe even boring them to death. Others counselors seem to be more natural, and this makes us reluctant to try. What's sinking us is comparing ourselves to others rather than relaxing into our own style. Authenticity and congruence is always effective, and it's much less work!

_____

_____

_____

_____

_____

_____

_____

_____

_____

_____

_____

_____

_____

_____

April 15 — Resentment

"I've taped a list to my bathroom mirror. It's my Most Violated List. . . Anger. I gave the finger to an ATM. You see, the ATM charged me a $1.75 fee for withdrawl. A dollar seventy-five? That's bananas. So I flipped off the screen. As Julie tells me, when you start making rude gestures to inanimate objects, it's time to work on your anger issues. Mine is not the shouting, pulsing-vein-in-the-forehead rage. Like my dad, I rarely raise my voice. My anger problem is more one of long-lasting resentment. It's a heap of real or perceived slights that eventually build up into a mountain of bitterness. . . get some perspective. . . I ask myself the question God asked Jonah. 'Do you do well to be angry?'. . .The world will not end. . . Mute your petty resentment."

A.J. Jacobs

Am I the only one who can relate to this rant? As Al-anon says, "How important is it?"

"We sometimes choose the most locked up, dark versions of the story, but what a good friend does is turn on the lights, open the window, and remind us that there are a whole lot of ways to tell the same story."

Shauna Niequist, Bittersweet: Thoughts on Change, Grace, and Learning the Hard Way.

There's an approach to counseling called Narrative Therapy that focuses on the stories we tell about our lives. It teaches us to re-tell the stories with more perspective and sometimes more realistically than our traumatized memory may allow. As we listen to the stories our clients share, we can look for the strengths, successes, overlooked opportunities and draw the client's attention to them. While we don't want to diminish their experience, we can gently reframe or suggest alternative perspectives. It's fun to hear a client say, "I never thought about it that way!"

_____

_____

_____

_____

_____

_____

_____

_____

_____

_____

_____

_____

_____

APRIL 17 — HUMILITY

"Be careful not to mistake insecurity and inadequacy for humility! Humility has nothing to do with the insecure and inadequate! Just like arrogance has nothing to do with greatness!"

C. JoyBell C.

Have you ever heard of "Secret Narcissists?" While narcissists crave attention recognition and have a strong sense of entitlement, secret narcissists pretend they are less-than to trigger other to recite their accomplishments and give them the spotlight they crave. When people are truly humble they are able to acknowledge their accomplishments without letting them define who they are. Humble people retain the mind of a learner, and are happy to share the spotlight with others. When is the last time you did a Tenth Step?

_____

_____

_____

_____

_____

_____

_____

_____

_____

_____

_____

_____

_____

_____

"When people are ready to, they change. They never do it before then, and sometimes they die before they get around to it. You can't make them change if they don't want to, just like when they do want to, you can't stop them."

Andy Warhol, Andy Warhol in His Own Words

Do you remember what motivated you to change when changing would cost you? Even recovery costs us – we leave lifestyles, friends, sometimes homes and careers. There has to be such a powerful reason to change that we will persist even when we have excuses not to. I can remember entering recovery in a whole new way because I thought I would die if I didn't. And I didn't want to die, so I was persistent. The challenge and fun in Motivational Interviewing is in unearthing the motivation with your clients. It can be unexpected and surprising, yet powerful once they put their finger on it. It keeps the job interesting!

April 19 — Rewards of recovery

"To sober up seems to many like making life "so serious," as if seriousness precluded joy, warmth, spontaneity and fun. But there can be a delusional, blind quality to non-sober festivities. To have our eyes open soberly with all our senses and memory intact allows some of the most rewarding, soul-nourishing, and long-lasting pleasures possible."

Alexandra Katehakis

"My life is over" is a fear every alcohol and drug counselor has been faced with. Clients imagine their lives filled only with meetings, Big Book studies, soda, and service. Everything they loved like concerts, traveling, and sports now seem unavailable due to sobriety, and it's no wonder they flee back into their drug of choice! We need to demonstrate with our own lives and attitudes that our lives in recovery are rich; that we travel, that we go to concerts and ball games. Everything that gave us joy is still available and now even more rewarding because we can fully participate.

_____

_____

_____

_____

_____

_____

_____

_____

_____

_____

_____

_____

"... the alcoholic is an extreme example of self-will run riot... Above everything, we alcoholics must get rid of selfishness. God makes that possible."

AA, 2001, p. 62

How true was this of you in your addiction? It was true in mine, though for women it can seem less obvious due to our Codependency. We can look over-giving, thoughtful, sacrificing . . . at the other side of all this giving is the anxiety that droves it and the resentment when we aren't appreciated for "all we do." It's profoundly selfish to have scripts in our relationships that others are supposed to follow, and to impose the "advice" we are so sure is best for people we love. Healthy love allows us to respect others enough to believe that they have a Higher Power, and it isn't us!

_____

_____

_____

_____

_____

_____

_____

_____

_____

_____

_____

_____

_____

_____

_____

April 21 — Cross-Addiction

"We must move in our recovery from one addiction to another for two major reasons: first, we have not recognized and treated the underlying addictive process, and second, we have not accurately isolated and focused upon the specific addictions."

Anne Wilson Schaef

Cross-addiction is a very real and underlying factor in relapse for so many of us. Dopamine seeking, our instinct is to "self-soothe" when leaving one addiction to another. Food, sex, spending, gambling, video games. . . there are so many ways to try to recapture the emotional numbness that we were seeking. It's the ability to "check out" that tempts even long-term recovering addicts and alcoholics, so it is immediately present for our clients. We need to stay alert to client distractions, such as "hooking up," starting drama, or using outrageous amounts of sugar in their coffee. Then again, maybe we need to watch our own coffee!

"When the Japanese mend broken objects, they aggrandize the damage by filling the cracks with gold. They believe that when something's suffered damage and has a history it becomes more beautiful."

Barbara Bloom

Isn't this a gorgeous analogy for what we do? We are able to see the value in the cracks and grooves in our clients, recognizing that there's wisdom in there to be unearthed. We know this is true when we reflect back on our own lives. There are times when we hear a nugget of wisdom come out of our mouths, wisdom we earned by taking a thorough look at ourselves and owning who we are. We fill client cracks with gold made of kindness, compassion, honest feedback, and service. Our role is precious.

_____

_____

_____

_____

_____

_____

_____

_____

_____

_____

_____

_____

_____

_____

_____

"Hard isn't it? Trying to stay strong for everyone around you, with a pasted on smile that quickly goes away when you're alone. I know it's tough trying to kill something that's on the inside, that eats you alive, and there's nothing you can do about it. No matter how hard you try, it just doesn't go away. I know it ain't easy, but I know things will get better."

Anonymous

What a brilliant description of early recovery – trying to stay strong for people who love you, and not speaking about your PAW symptoms, hoping that eventually you'll feel better. This is what white knuckling feels like, and our only hope is to reach out and ask for the help and support we desperately need. How about you? Are you pasting on a smile and "faking normal" when inside you feel like you are wasting away? If you are, please seek help today. You deserve the same care and healing that you are offering to your clients. If you're not in this position, take steps today to avoid feeling like this.

_____

_____

_____

_____

_____

_____

_____

_____

_____

_____

"Submitting seemed to me a lot like giving up. If God gave us the strength to bail- the gumption to try and save ourselves- isn't that what he wanted us to do?"

Jeannette Walls, Half Broke Horses

The surrender piece of program can be so hard for our clients. Most of us have an instinct to hold on, force our will, manipulate and bargain. It's not just our attempts to control drugs and alcohol that we surrender, but later we have to surrender our control over our character defects. The ego doesn't give up easily, and resists losing or being defeated. That's why it's so important to reframe surrender to emphasize the empowerment that comes when we stop fighting. We can then use our energy differently, focusing it in ways to grow and heal. Timmen Cermak calls it "Winning through Losing."

APRIL 25 — ACCEPTANCE

"If you want reality to be different than it is, you might as well try to teach a cat to bark."

Byron Katie

Okay, many of us have worked incredibly hard to change reality, even when it wasn't in our power to do so. We want what we want, and God knows Codependents are not quitters! If we thought we could get someone we love sober by trying to teach a cat to bark we would! Acceptance can be painful initially, and maybe we're afraid that if we accept reality on its own terms we'll lose control. We can't trust events to work out without our involvement. This is because we have a vision of how things "should be" and ignore other outcomes, possibilities that could actually provide more joy and more serenity than our picture ever could.

_____

_____

_____

_____

_____

_____

_____

_____

_____

_____

_____

_____

_____

"Health is the natural condition. When sickness occurs, it is a sign that Nature has gone off course because of a physical or mental imbalance. The road to health for everyone is through moderation, harmony, and a 'sound mind in a sound body'."

Jostein Gaarder, Sophie's World

We sacrificed our health for years using and drinking, or living under the chronic stress of relationship chaos. Moderation is confusing to most of us, living in the world of all-or-nothing for so many years. Even with years of sobriety we still might be missing the "moderation gene" and need to monitor ourselves and do regular check in's with people we trust. Left to our own devices we forget we have limits, and can run ourselves into the ground. Our body pays the price, protesting gently and if we ignore us, breaking down to get our attention!

_____

_____

_____

_____

_____

_____

_____

_____

_____

_____

_____

_____

"Stressed souls need the reassuring rhythm of self-nurturing rituals".

Sarah Ban Breathnach Simple Abundance

What kind of soothing rituals do you have to bring your adrenal system down when you're stressed? One of the things I do with clients is help them create a Sensory Tool Box, a collection of sensory items that can help them calm themselves when they are agitated.

Favorite smells

Favorite fabrics for touch

Favorite tastes

Favorite Sights

Favorite Sounds

Collecting a soft shirt or blanket, a scented candle, or calming music can be the self-care plan you need after a really hard day at the treatment center!

_____

_____

_____

_____

_____

_____

_____

_____

_____

_____

"Sometimes we motivate ourselves by thinking of what we want to become. Sometimes we motivate ourselves by thinking about who we don't ever want to be again. Everything we do is part of who we are. How we choose to use those memories, to motivate or to submit is entirely up to us."

Shane Niemeyer - The Hurt Artist

Have you ever heard the phrase, "It could be that the purpose of your life is only to serve as a warning to others"? Some of us can relate to this more than others, and you've probably had the experience of an older client in the center pointing out to younger clients that they're the ghost of Christmas future if the "kids" don't stop using. It's true that the memory of our last use, our last arrest, our last CPS report can motivate us to do what we need to do to say sober and never have that kind of pain again.

_____

_____

_____

_____

_____

_____

_____

_____

_____

_____

_____

_____

_____

April 29 — Moving forward

"Even if you're on the right track you'll get run over if you just sit there."

Will Rogers

Sometimes we get comfortable in our routine and we stop growing. We get lazy about keeping up with our CEU's and have to grab them in a panic at the last minute. We stay in relationships or work situation that are "okay," and we ignore the voice inside of us that tells us we've outgrown the situation and could do better. It's the nature of life that it keeps moving forward, with or without us. Time passes as we stay frozen planning. We can help our clients remember this; that treatment is their chance to move forward with life rather than treading water the way they have for years. When they finally do start moving forward they will have to grieve the time they've lost and still keep moving.

_____

_____

_____

_____

_____

_____

_____

_____

_____

_____

_____

_____

_____

"We labor under the great delusion that we are in control. Silly humans."

Toni Sorenson

It IS human to want control, especially over our own lives. This is a healthy sign, a sign that developmentally we learned the importance of initiative and the ability to make choices on our own behalf. When clients are fighting us in treatment, trying to run their own program, it's not the instinct that's the problem. It's their lack of awareness over their inability to control their alcohol and drug use that creates the flaw in their planning. The decision to surrender THIS lack of control will increase the strength of their future decision making and they'll have increased control over their own lives. When I have to drive with eyes in the back of my head because of my suspended license, I'm truly not in control of my life.

_____

_____

_____

_____

_____

_____

_____

_____

_____

_____

_____

_____

MAY 1 — IDENTIFICATION

"I used to think I was the strangest person in the world but then I thought there are so many people in the world, there must be someone just like me who feels bizarre and flawed in the same ways I do. I would imagine her, and imagine that she must be out there thinking of me too. Well, I hope that if you are out there and read this and know that, yes, it's true I'm here, and I'm just as strange as you."

Frida Kahlo

Frida Kahlo turned a devastating accident and chronic pain into art, sometimes dark but vibrant art. Survival can bring out strange behaviors and make us a little "quirky." The healing power of identification is the secret to Twelve Step success. It's the reason so much of addiction treatment is group therapy based. We laugh in the rooms when others wouldn't see the humor, and we're able to see with compassion what others might judge. It can be comforting that other people recognize the craziness in our thoughts and decision making.

_____

_____

_____

_____

_____

_____

_____

_____

_____

_____

_____

MAY 2 — GRATITUDE

"Be thankful for what you have; you'll end up having more. If you concentrate on what you don't have, you will never, ever have enough"

Oprah Winfrey

Have you ever given a workshop and then read though the evaluations? 25 of them comment on your preparation and the benefits, and then there's always that one that gives you a 1 or 2. I once had someone write about the way my slip didn't match my skirt, and how she was much more professional than me. Ouch!!! Recovery wisdom tells us to practice gratitude. It's certainly my experience that the more kindness I offer the more kindness I receive. The more irritable I am, the more crabby people I seem to run-into! It's important to notice the wins, notice the resources you DO have, and the people who DO love you. When our vision becomes too narrow our attitude can begin to shift.

MAY 3 — COUNTER-TRANSFERENCE

"Those who educate us can never be forgotten. Wherever we are, they will always be in our heart and mind."

Lailah Gifty Akita

Our clients affect us, change us, in unexpected ways. We have the chance to learn about ourselves every day as we walk them through their dilemmas and empathize with their fears. Counter-transference is really instructive. The clients that are most annoying, needy, knuckle-headed, and willing capture our attention and force us to grow. There are still clients I saw many years ago that come to mind from time to time. They usually challenged me and touched my heart with their story. On occasion their story was my story, and in supporting them I heard the reminders I needed to hear.

May 4 — Recognizing co-workers

"Being in the habit of saying "Thank you," of making sure that people receive attention so they know you value them, of not presuming that people will always be there--this is a good habit, regardless...make sure to give virtual and actual high-fives to those who rock and rock hard."

Sarah Wendell, Everything I Know About Love I Learned from Romance Novels

It's important to recognize our co-workers who all too often are not being recognized by their clients or even supervisors. Administrators have different responsibilities, and this makes them sometimes unaware of the day-to-day operations of the facility. When you witness an insightful comment, or overhear clients commenting favorably about another counselor, make a point to share it with them. It's also okay to share your successes and enjoy your successes. The combination of both approaches creates collegiality and keeps everyone on the same team.

_____
_____
_____
_____
_____
_____
_____
_____
_____
_____
_____

"Nothing happens on its own, you have to make things happen. If you really want to come out of your stressful situation than you need to take action. Unless you stand up for yourself and take action, the problem is not going to get away. Let fear of failure shouldn't stop you from taking action"

Subodh Gupta, Stress Management a Holistic Approach

We have to be part of the solution or we can slide into victimhood. This was a position many of us had for years. The advantage to being a victim is that you're absolved of any responsibility, and if you were good at this you could get other people to take responsibility for you! We watch this game with our clients on a daily basis, terrified of owning their part of the problem because they're afraid of the change it would require. If I never try I never have to fail.

_____

_____

_____

_____

_____

_____

_____

_____

_____

_____

_____

_____

_____

_____

MAY 6 — BOUNDARIES

"Blessed are those who give without remembering. And blessed are those who take without forgetting"

Bernard Meltzer

People who are drawn to the counseling field, particularly the addiction field, more often than not have addiction in their family if not in their own lives. We've been on the giving side many times, over-giving in an effort to be valued and earn our worth. It can be hard for us to give without keeping a silent score card, and the lopsidedness of our relationships eventually triggers an eruption of resentment. Many of our clients were codependent before they were ever addicted, and may have been self-medicating their codependency all these years. Boundaries are essential for their sobriety and essential for our emotional sobriety.

"The test we must set for ourselves is not to march alone but to march in such a way that others will wish to join us."

Hubert H. Humphrey

I was reminded about the "attraction and not promotion" principle of the Twelve Step program. It's also a way to lead our lives; trying to be the kind of person other people respect and want to be. On the other hand, we know that our more admirable traits come and go and we're always a work in progress. The art of living includes the ability to rebound, not being perfect. Actually, perfect people are really annoying and hard to be close to. When someone's humanity is present, especially combined with competence and kindness, it's an attractive package indeed!

_____

_____

_____

_____

_____

_____

_____

_____

_____

_____

_____

_____

_____

_____

_____

_____

_____

MAY 8 — PATIENCE

"We must be content to grow slowly. Most of us will still barely be at the beginning of our recovery by the time we die. But that is better than killing ourselves pretending to be healthy."

Simon Tugwell

The perspective offered here requires a great deal of patience with ourselves. Some of us are naturally quiet, observant, and able to wait for long periods of time. We're just built that way – were probably like that as children. Others of us were born running instead of walking. Our primary focus is on speed before accuracy, so our approach to recovery is the same. We want God to eliminate our character defects NOW. We want the spirituality of an old-timer when we have 3 years clean! Throwing ourselves into our recovery without balance is a recipe to burn-out and drop-out. Even worse, it can lead us to a case of the "F***it's" and relapse. Patience with ourselves can save our lives!

"I have come to accept the feeling of not knowing where I am going. And I have trained myself to love it. Because it is only when we are suspended in mid-air with no landing in sight, that we force our wings to unravel and alas begin our flight. And as we fly, we still may not know where we are going to. But the miracle is in the unfolding of the wings. You may not know where you're going, but you know that so long as you spread your wings, the winds will carry you."

C. JoyBell C.

There is so much trust implied here, impossible without a Higher Power. Many of us felt like we were floating in mid-air most of childhoods, with no safety net. Our parents and caregivers were preoccupied with their own survival, and we learned early to trust ourselves. We became our own higher power. The trusting process is a long one for many of us, and we can empathize as we watch our clients struggle with the 3rd Step.

"Don't ever feel bad that someone couldn't give you all of their heart. Be grateful that you can take the least complicated part of their soul with you, wherever you go. This is more than some people will ever have."

Shannon L. Alder

We were speaking of trust yesterday. Not only do clients struggle with the 3rd Step, they're also reluctant to trust us. This can be irritating at times because we KNOW they should trust us, we're the good guys, right? Most of our clients have encountered people in the system over time, and not all of them were supportive. In fact, we're probably just one more person in their life saying we want to "help." It's extremely important that we find out how they define their problem, and it may or may not include abstinence. The key is forming an effective alliance!

_____

_____

_____

_____

_____

_____

_____

_____

_____

_____

_____

_____

_____

_____

"Vulnerability scares most of us because we've been taught that FEELING our feelings is a sign of "over-sensitivity and weakness". We've taught ourselves to "numb" our feelings because they are too painful.

We arrive at vulnerability when we allow ourselves to FEEL rather than think our feelings.

It's an inside job of excavating away all the "stuff" that is in the way of reaching our heart, where love and vulnerability live."

Marlene Milner

Culture and gender inform the way we define weakness and strength. Traditionally, women have more permission to feel than men, and traditionally men have more permission to be openly angry. All of us are afraid of exposure, though some of us have more practice than others. Recovery gives us practice being vulnerable and honest in a whole new way. This is why we're "grateful" alcoholics and Alanons'.

_____

_____

_____

_____

_____

_____

_____

_____

_____

_____

_____

MAY 12 — SELF-COMPASSION

"To the people who love you, you are beautiful already. This is not because they're blind to your shortcomings but because they so clearly see your soul. Your shortcomings then dim by comparison. The people who care about you are willing to let you be imperfect and beautiful, too."

Victoria Moran, Lit From Within: Tending Your Soul For
Lifelong Beauty

Pia Mellody states that "Love is holding someone in warm personal regard despite harmful impact on you. Harmful means when they act outside your value system." It takes a lot of self-awareness to love someone in this way, to continue to stay connected with someone when they're acting out their imperfections. How well do you hold yourself in warm regard when you notice your shortcomings? When we are able to extend compassion to ourselves it naturally spills out into other relationships in our lives.

"Highly sensitive people are too often perceived as weaklings or damaged goods. To feel intensely is not a symptom of weakness, it is the trademark of the truly alive and compassionate. It is not the empath who is broken, it is society that has become dysfunctional and emotionally disabled. There is no shame in expressing your authentic feelings. Those who are at times described as being a 'hot mess' or having 'too many issues' are the very fabric of what keeps the dream alive for a more caring, humane world. Never be ashamed to let your tears shine a light in this world."

Anthon St. Maarten

Some of us grew up being told we were too sensitive or 'crybabies." Addicts and alcoholics are known to be very sensitive, so numbing with alcohol and drugs makes sense. Recovering people are often afraid that if they let themselves cry, they'll never stop! We can help clients trust that we don't cry forever and tears uncertainty don't kill us. They heal us.

_____

_____

_____

_____

_____

_____

_____

_____

_____

_____

_____

_____

MAY 14 — ANGER

"A belligerent samurai, an old Japanese tale goes, once challenged a Zen master to explain the concept of heaven and hell.

The monk replied with scorn, "You're nothing but a lout - I can't waste my time with the likes of you!"

His very honor attacked, the samurai flew into a rage and, pulling his sword from its scabbard, yelled "I could kill you for your impertinence."

"That," the monk calmly replied, "is hell."

Startled at seeing the truth in what the master pointed out about the fury that had him in its grip, the samurai calmed down, sheathed his sword, and bowed, thanking the monk for the insight.

"And that," said the monk "is heaven."

> Daniel Goleman, *Emotional Intelligence: Why It Can Matter More Than IQ*

_____

_____

_____

_____

_____

_____

_____

_____

_____

_____

_____

_____

"The leaders I met, whatever walk of life they were from, whatever institutions they were presiding over, always referred back to the same failure - something that happened to them that was personally difficult, even traumatic, something that made them feel that desperate sense of hitting bottom--as something they thought was almost a necessity. It's as if at that moment the iron entered their soul; that moment created the resilience that leaders need."

Warren Bennis

Psychologist Virginia Satir described us as leaders of change in our role as a counselor. The client or family is confused, lost, and knows that their solutions haven't worked. We are able to lead them out of the desert because we've wandered in the desert ourselves. We developed the iron resolve that allows us to keep offering to be of service even when clients aren't convinced they NEED our service. Rather than be discouraged, we simply wait.

May 16 — Influencing others

"The things we do outlast our mortality. The things we do are like monuments that people build to honor heroes after they've died. They're like the pyramids that the Egyptians built to honor the pharaohs. Only instead of being made of stone, they're made out of the memories people have of you."

R.J. Palacio, Wonder

When you think back to people who've affected your life, what kind of memories are enshrined there? We influence the effect we have on our clients, including the memories of us they will carry with them long after treatment has ended. It's interesting to me that people will often remember the small kindnesses, the quick story you told about yourself to make a point, or the way you handle a difficult client in group. They remember these moments far more than the fabulous psychoeducation lecture on brain chemistry or the discharge plan we wrote that was going to keep them sober.

_____

_____

_____

_____

_____

_____

_____

_____

_____

_____

"Sometimes we have to meet people where they are, Ollie. Honor their desires, regardless of our own."

Tess Hilmo, With a Name like Love

We know that people enter treatment at different stages of change, and in some cases we work in harm reduction systems that don't require abstinence. If we're in recovery ourselves this can make us very uncomfortable, believing that taking "life on life's terms" is the only healthy path to recovery. Individualized treatment requires us to meet clients where they are in their recovery process, and sometimes this means they aren't ready to enter the recovery process the way we would define it. Our job is to help the client meet the goals THEY have for their treatment episode which may mean "stay out of jail" or "keep my job" rather than sobriety.

_____

_____

_____

_____

_____

_____

_____

_____

_____

_____

_____

_____

_____

Sometimes we go along, thinking
"Ah, this is it - this is what true peace feels like..."
Then, in a moment of grace, something shifts in our hearts,
and in awestruck wonder, we whisper,
"Oh my, I just didn't know there could more..."

Kate Mullane Robertson

When our lives have been hard the bar we set for our expectations can be set fairly low. We think he's a good man because he "doesn't hit us" not knowing that this is STANDARD in a healthy relationship. Maybe it's an upgrade for us given our background. So, clients may have low expectations for themselves seen in under earning, staying with someone they don't love because it's the "best they can get," or struggling with depression unnecessarily not believing that medication will help; "It's just the way I am." We need to check our expectation for our lives also. It's hard to be encouraging about what life offers if yours is empty.

May 19 — Sarcasm

"He announces that lately he keeps losing things. "Like your wife and child," I want to say, but don´t. At forty, I´ve learned not to say everything clever, not to score every point."

Suzanne Finnamore, Split: A Memoir of Divorce

There are times when we have a desire to be flip with our clients or coworkers. We have an impulse to be sarcastic or to imitate them. Did you know that in Latin, sarcasm means "tearing of flesh"? It's a particularly nasty form of humor because for it to be funny, someone has to be the butt of the joke. Everyone but them thinks it's hilarious! When people are in early recovery they're often pretty concrete thinkers, so may not always know we are joking or get the joke in a group situation. This makes them more vulnerable to misunderstandings and hurt feelings.

_____

_____

_____

_____

_____

_____

_____

_____

_____

_____

_____

_____

_____

_____

_____

"Hope distracts you from pain - it's pain with red lipstick on to seduce you."

Kevin James Moore, The Go-Go Girl

I loved this image! We need the red lipstick of hope to sustain us through early recovery. Our clients need a realistic basis for hope, a plan with goals they can realistically achieve. We often witness the "pink cloud" effect that makes them grandiose in their planning when they feel physically more energetic. It's hard because we don't want to take away their enthusiasm, and at the same time our experience makes us aware of the red flags. Listening to the success of other clients who are further along in their recovery, as well as hearing from clients who are struggling, can speak louder to them than anything we can say. This is the beauty of clients at different points in their process, who are able to influence each other in positive ways.

_____

_____

_____

_____

_____

_____

_____

_____

_____

_____

_____

_____

"Mindfulness helps us get better at seeing the difference between what's happening and the stories we tell ourselves about what's happening, stories that get in the way of direct experience. Often such stories treat a fleeting state of mind as if it were our entire and permanent self."

Sharon Salzberg, Real Happiness: The Power of Meditation

Mindfulness allows us to observe our thoughts as they pass through our mind. The trick is to not attach to the thoughts and make them our reality. We have so many stories about our life, as though we were watching a movie. Sometimes when client's talk about their lives they sound as though they are reporting on a life they've observed rather than lived. This is one effect of trauma – a distancing that makes the feelings that could be so overwhelming bearable. We need to pay attention to our stories and talk to others to sort out the real from the unreal.

MAY 22 — RESILIENCE

"The greatest discovery is to find a hero within oneself that will choose life over death; and fight for hope through despair to possess the will to live."

Ellen J. Barrier

When we're in the disease, we're in the twilight between life and death on a daily basis. Despite our self-abuse, we don't die. On the other hand, we're not really living. To stay sober over the long-term we have to have a reason to live. This means we have to enough energy and stubbornness to push our way through the bumps that are inevitable in life. There has to be a driving passion that helps us stay resilient and do what it takes to keep us sober. The truth is we can't do this ourselves, we're going to have to ask for help and to keep an open mind when help is offered!

_____

_____

_____

_____

_____

_____

_____

_____

_____

_____

_____

_____

_____

_____

_____

MAY 23 — SELF-COMPASSION

"An important aspect of self-compassion is to be able to empathically hold both parts of ourselves--the self that regrets a past action and the self that took the action in the first place."

Marshall Rosenberg

This reminds me of the phrase, "We shall not regret the past nor wish to shut the door on it" that we've heard so often in program. It takes a lot of energy to ruminate about the past. The pictures loop and loop through our mind, and takes up space for new thoughts and new insight. We're locked in. Self-compassion lets us out. We make the best decisions we can with the information we have at the time. When we're loaded our judgment is impaired and we make horrendous choices. Most of them are self-destructive, so or amends begin with amends to ourselves for our lack of self-care and self-protection. The best amends are living ones, and we can begin with self-care today.

_____

_____

_____

_____

_____

_____

_____

_____

_____

_____

_____

_____

"But no one is easier to delude than a parent; they see only what they wish to see."

Karen Joy Fowler, We Are All Completely Beside Ourselves

Working with family members in a treatment program has its own set of challenges. Parents, like clients, have their own stage of change process, and often don't see the larger picture. They don't understand the disease, and often have unrealistic expectations. They often have distorted pictures of the addict/alcoholic in their lives, and don't see their role in the addiction and recovery process. Our role is to provide gentle education and support about the changes that need to happen for the family to heal, and to do this without blaming them. This can be hard if the counselor hasn't addressed their own family of origin issues. Reactivity with family members is a signal that we have work to do.

_____

_____

_____

_____

_____

_____

_____

_____

_____

_____

_____

_____

"Service is a smile. It is an acknowledging wave, a reaching handshake, a friendly wink, and a warm hug. It's these simple acts that matter most, because the greatest service to a human soul has always been the kindness of recognition."

Richelle E. Goodrich, Smile Anyway: Quotes, Verse, &
Grumblings for Every Day of the Year

Some of us are natural healers just being who we are. When people are in our presence they seem to relax and quiet themselves. Maybe we want to BE this kind of person; the kind of person who gives the other person our full attention. We want to be non-judgmental and see through to who people are regardless of what they've done. It's easier to be this kind of person if we've met this kind of person. We need these kind of people in our lives, people who extend love and acceptance simply because of who we are and not what we do.

_____

_____

_____

_____

_____

_____

_____

_____

_____

_____

_____

"But this revolutionary act of treating ourselves tenderly can begin to undo the aversive messages of a lifetime."

Tara Brach, Radical Acceptance: Embracing Your Life With the Heart of a Buddha

Many of us have decades of messages we have been given about who we are, what we can accomplish, and what we deserve. We may still be acting on those messages – our clients certainly are. The only way we're going to heal those old, outdates messages is to begin to treat ourselves as though they aren't true. Apply for the job even though we think we "don't deserve it." We can let ourselves rest even though have been told resting means we're "lazy." Fortunately we don't have to feel better to treat ourselves as though we matter.

_____

_____

_____

_____

_____

_____

_____

_____

_____

_____

_____

_____

_____

_____

_____

"The fact is that we have no way of knowing if the person who we think we are is at the core of our being. Are you a decent girl with the potential to someday become an evil monster, or are you an evil monster that thinks it's a decent girl?"
"Wouldn't I know which one I was?"

"Good God, no. The lies we tell other people are nothing to the lies we tell ourselves."

Derek Landy, Death Bringer

Isn't this true! The self-deception of addiction begins with the lies we tell ourselves about how well we're "managing" our lives. We can develop the ability to become open-minded, willing, and honest. We can do this through the Twelve Steps or another support system that holds us accountable for who we are in the world. We may not have denial about alcohol, but what about our control issues?

_____

_____

_____

_____

_____

_____

_____

_____

_____

_____

_____

_____

_____

_____

_____

MAY 28 — RUTS

"The only difference between a rut and a grave are the dimensions."

Ellen Glasgow

Isn't this true? But a rut can be so seductive. When the chaos of addiction subsides, and we start to get used to the lack of drama, we can start to value predictability. In fact, we can value it so much that we become afraid to disturb the status quo – afraid to "screw with what's working" and one day drifts into the next. When was the last time you took a look at your life and challenged yourself to learn something new? Do you travel or have new experiences? It's important to keep growing in our recovery.

_____

_____

_____

_____

_____

_____

_____

_____

_____

_____

_____

_____

_____

_____

_____

_____

_____

"Nothing that we despise in other men is inherently absent from ourselves. We must learn to regard people less in the light of what they do or don't do, and more in light of what they suffer."

Dietrich Bonhoeffer

This is harder than it sounds. People affect us by what they DO and it can be hard to keep a detached and spiritual perspective. Clients can be incredibly frustrating, and when they're acting out we can forget the anxiety or suffering that may lie beneath their behavior. Our tendency is to take it personally, and begin to attach labels to them like "borderline," or "sociopath." While these labels may or may not apply, using them to define clients creates distance between people. It's important to stay aware of where clients come from, remembering that they may reflect a pattern generations deep.

_____

_____

_____

_____

_____

_____

_____

_____

_____

_____

_____

_____

_____

MAY 30 — BELONGING

"Everyone is a genius. But if you judge a fish on it's ability to climb a tree, it will spend it's whole life believing it is stupid"

Albert Einstein

Have you ever seen a client with their family and thought, "How did they get in that family?" Some of us can relate to feeling out of sync with our family of origin, which usually saw us as "wrong." Being slow and deliberate in a fast-paced, loud family can be perceived as a "problem," However in a slower, quieter family you would've fit right in. Part of recovery is finding our "tribe" which may not be our original "tribe." Al-anon was this tribe for me, and I remember being tearful with relief as I listened to other members and felt like I belonged. This feeling is crucial for addicts and alcoholics who often feel like everyone else was born with the manual, "how to do life," but them.

_____
_____
_____
_____
_____
_____
_____
_____
_____
_____
_____
_____

MAY 31 — TEARS

"There is a sacredness in tears. They are not the mark of weaken but of power. They speak more eloquently than ten thousand tongues. They are messengers of overwhelming grief. . . and unspeakable love.

Washington Irving

We may have grown up in families where tears were a sign of weakness that could be exploited by other family members. We may have spent our lives developing a strong outer shell that we have been carrying for so long we believe it's who we are, not a wall we've built. When clients begin to shed their substantial shells, and their soft underbelly peeks out, they can be overwhelmed by their tears. They may be afraid they will never quit crying. We have the privilege to witness to their pain and sit still with them while they heal in front of us. Advice is not needed here, just a quiet presence.

_____

_____

_____

_____

_____

_____

_____

_____

_____

_____

_____

_____

_____

JUNE 1 — INFLUENCING OTHERS

"The healing of ourselves as healers has to take place first. Bringing ourselves to wholeness, we become more sensitive to other people. In the change of consciousness that happens within us, we bring about change of consciousness in those around us and in the planet itself."

Marion Woodman

One of the more rewarding aspects of working in the addiction field is how rapidly we can see shifts in not just the addicts but the addicts' family. It's been said that every alcoholic/addict affects at least 6 people, so this means every time an addict heals they affect 6 people. The recovering community affects the larger community, and it's an honor to be part of that healing circle. The healing starts with us as we grow in our own recovery. As we continue to hone our personal compassion for ourselves and others, we impact the community even more. One person DOES make a difference, something important for our clients to grasp as well.

_____

_____

_____

_____

_____

_____

_____

_____

_____

_____

_____

"I have been all things unholy. If God can work through me, he can work through anyone."

St. Francis of Assisi have been all things unholy

The story of St. Francis is a powerful one. An indulged son of a rich family, he received a vision on the way to war, and became touched by the plight of the poor. Poverty was essential to his mission. Despite this, he was aware of his humanity and behavior in his youth and maintained an exquisite sense of humility. If St. Francis can see his challenges of pride and willfulness, we can too. All of us are human before we are anything else. Our humanity is both our strength and our weakness. Our humanity is why we need others, why we function best in community. Our weakness IS our strength. Timmen Cermak calls this "Winning through Losing."

_____

_____

_____

_____

_____

_____

_____

_____

_____

_____

_____

_____

_____

_____

June 3 — Hope

"Do not let your fire go out, spark by irreplaceable spark, in the hopeless swamps of the approximate, the not-quite, the not-yet, the not-at-all. Do not let the hero in your soul perish, in lonely frustration for the life you deserved, but have never been able to reach. Check your road and the nature of your battle. The world you desired can be won. It exists, it is real, it is possible, it is yours."

Ayn Rand Quote for Overcoming Addiction

Our fear of wanting and hoping can be paralyzing. Our lives may have been a series of broken promises or disappointing endings, and when we continue to hope we expose ourselves to more heartbreak. On the other had if we don't hope we will not be able to push ourselves forward. One of our primary functions as counselors is to support the hope that our clients may be afraid of, and if we're going to sell them on trusting the future we're going to have to be living as though this is true for ourselves. Are you letting yourself hope?

_____

_____

_____

_____

_____

_____

_____

_____

_____

_____

_____

"I long to accomplish a great and noble task, but it is my chief duty to accomplish humble tasks as though they were great and noble."

Helen Keller

There are parts of our job that are annoying and tiring. We entered the counseling field to work with people, to comfort people, and we didn't sign up for all of this paperwork! Sometimes we're short-handed and we're asked to participate in the treatment program in ways that aren't "our job." In my role as a counselor, even as Clinical Director, I've taken out the trash, cooked dinner, and taken clients to the doctor. In treatment we need to do what needs to be done, and hiding behind our job title may not be practical. While it's important that we do the Twelve Core functions we've been hired to do, you may need to occasionally do the UA or grab some toilet paper while you're out.

_____

_____

_____

_____

_____

_____

_____

_____

_____

_____

_____

_____

"If you learn to really sit with loneliness and embrace it for the gift that it is...an opportunity to get to know YOU, to learn how strong you really are, to depend on no one but YOU for your happiness...you will realize that a little loneliness goes a LONG way in creating a richer, deeper, more vibrant and colorful YOU."

Mandy Hale, The Single Woman: Life, Love, and a Dash of Sass

It's common for clients to be anxious when alone. In fact, they may have used alcohol or drugs to avoid their feelings of aloneness when in relationships. The temptation to enter a relationship, even in treatment, to fill the void alcohol leaves is a normal one. We can encourage our clients to experiment with aloneness, even for an hour, while in treatment. We can offer an opportunity to learn to appreciate their own company, and discover that they can be the best relationship they will ever have!

_____

_____

_____

_____

_____

_____

_____

_____

_____

_____

_____

_____

"Did your mom ever tell you, 'If you can't say something nice, don't say anything'? She was right—and talking nicely also applies when you're talking to yourself, even inside your head. (339)"

> *Victoria Moran, Younger by the Day: 365 Ways to Rejuvenate Your Body and Revitalize Your Spirit*

The committee in our head can be pretty snarky. They can use power point to illustrate our conversational blunders, our awkward moments, our embarrassing mistakes. This is why in recovery we sometimes hear that entering our own head alone is a bad idea, because we're entering a "bad neighborhood!" Quieting the committee requires us to pull the power plug on the LCD projector, and listen to people who are supportive. We can even invite new committee members in, members who can counteract the negative ruminating thoughts when they start. Kindness to ourselves begins with us.

_____

_____

_____

_____

_____

_____

_____

_____

_____

_____

_____

_____

June 7 — Live with intention

Live with intention.
Walk to the edge.
Listen hard.
Practice wellness.
Play with abandon.
Laugh.
Choose with no regret.
Appreciate your friends.
Continue to learn.
Do what you love.
Live as if this is all there is.

Mary Anne Radmacher

What if this is all there is? That we only get one shot, and the clock's ticking? When we become aware that this is true, it can lend urgency and intention to our lives. We begin to examine our lives in the light of our value system – am I living the life that I pictured for myself? Playing is central to wellness, and this means we need to be willing to lose control of our "image" and be willing to be silly and not self-conscious.

_____

_____

_____

_____

_____

_____

_____

_____

_____

_____

"People are hungry for messages of hope and life. What are you broadcasting?"

Morgan Brittany

How much feedback do you invite into your life? You can sometimes tell a lot about you by listening to the people around you. Do they gossip? Are they snarky? Are they stoned? Are they cheating on their wives?

We'll drift toward those who are most comfortable for us, and it's important that there are still people in our lives growing, maybe even ahead of us, so we're pulled forward. When we work in treatment we are surrounded by the early disease, so may begin to feel like we have "arrived." This can be dangerous for our sobriety and serenity.

JUNE 9 — SHAME

"Shame is guilt in overdrive. If it helps think of the difference between shame and guilt as this: shame says "I'm bad, I'm flawed", guilt says "what I did was harmful to myself and/or others, and I can do better than that". Thoughts of healthy, unbiased guilt are how you converse with your conscience, while feelings of shame don't even let the conversation begin."

Renee Bledsoe

There is a neurology to shame. Our fight or fight system gets triggered, and we either move forward or move away from the shaming experience or person. We feel really little and don't see our options. Guilt keeps us from being sociopaths! We know that we impact people and we can create a bridge to make it right. It may be too late to make it right with the original person, but we can make living amends and make it right going forward.

_____

_____

_____

_____

_____

_____

_____

_____

_____

_____

_____

_____

_____

June 10 — Self-Pity

It's not a problem. There are people out there with much worse problems than mine. -Cynthia
"Doesn't make yours any more fun to bear."-Liza
"No. But it does help with the self-pity."- Cynthia"

Jennifer Crusie, Bet Me

It's strange how self-pity can creep up on me. There are times when I lose my perspective and the stumbling blocks in my life appear enormous. So I want to hide in bed with fig newton's and read murder mysteries. Does this sound familiar? The key is loss of perspective and self-absorption. This is one of the many reasons working with others is so vital for my sanity. Our clients provide us with perspective on a daily basis as we remember where we've been and see where we are. There is much to be grateful for!

JUNE 11 — ACCEPTANCE

"But of course these conjectures as to why God does what He does are probably of no more value than my dog's ideas of what I am up to when I sit and read."

C.S. Lewis, Reflections on the Psalms

This made me grin, as I immediately thought of how hard we try to make sense out of things, to see the meaning in situations as they're happening. Many of us are attached to a need to understand things, and twist and turn in our sleep wrestling to explain what cannot be explained. It reminds me of family members who spend hours pondering what the alcoholic was "thinking' when he got arrested. He wasn't thinking at all! Sometimes, when we're lucky, we see the "sense" in events after time has passed. We can see the unfolding consequences of a decision we made or an act someone took that blew our lives up. We have to accept what we might not ever understand because our suffering is in the struggle.

_____

_____

_____

_____

_____

_____

_____

_____

_____

_____

_____

_____

"There are those among us who have erred, deeply and significantly. Who have wounded the world and broken themselves. The worst of them lose themselves in their errors. The best of them crawl back, one foot at a time, and seek to amend their breaches. That is the way of the brave."

Chloe Neill, Wild Things

Recovery requires a lot of courage. Much more courage than remaining addicted and dying in our disease. Repairing a broken marriage, or making a long-avoided amends also takes courage. Being honest with ourselves about ourselves is a courageous act when so many people in the world remain entrenched in their denial and would co-sign us if we wanted to blame. Counselors hold themselves to a higher ethical standard than other people, and this can be a burden. But our effectiveness depends on it – denial is not an option. Otherwise we could be taxi driver and keep all of our issues!

_____
_____
_____
_____
_____
_____
_____
_____
_____
_____

June 13 — Change

"When we least expect it, life sets us a challenge to test our courage and willingness to change; at such a moment, there is no point in pretending that nothing has happened or in saying that we are not yet ready. The challenge will not wait. Life does not look back. A week is more than enough time for us to decide whether or not to accept our destiny."

Paulo Coelho, The Devil and Miss Prym

In recovery we often refer to the "window of opportunity" when an addict has a moment of clarity and recognizes that their life is out of control. We have other moments like this. The moment when we get a proposal, a job offer, an opportunity to travel, pregnancy . . . moments when our lives will change dramatically if we move forward. We are required to move in whatever direction we choose without a guarantee or contract. Supportive loved ones and wise mentors can stand by us and give us courage. It's hard to face life in isolation.

_____

_____

_____

_____

_____

_____

_____

_____

_____

_____

JUNE 14 — SURRENDER

"Whoever loves becomes humble. Those who love have, so to speak, pawned a part of their narcissism."

Sigmund Freud

Narcissism is often misunderstood. We have to have enough healthy narcissism to believe we have the ability to take on challenges in life. We develop healthy narcissism by being seen and heard accurately as children – to be mirrored in our parents' eyes as being wanted and valued. However, too much narcissism results in a need to be seen, to be the center of everyone and everything. Surrendering the need to be seen in order SEE someone else, hear someone else, compromise and negotiate is crucial to developing intimacy. Successful counselors have enough narcissism to feel competent and surrender it enough to enter the other person's reality and have empathy.

"You can't save others from themselves because those who make a perpetual muddle of their lives don't appreciate your interfering with the drama they've created. They want your poor-sweet-baby sympathy, but they don't want to change."

Sue Grafton, T is for Trespass

Have you worked with clients and coworkers whose lives appear to be one train wreck after another? Yet, attempts to support better choices quickly dissolve into playing, "Yes, but. . ." and they resist making different choices. This can be hard on us as helpers, because we feel like we aren't making a dent in the denial and chaos. This is a good time to remember the "planting the seed" theory of our work. The truth is we may never know how we've impacted our clients unless we run into them in a meeting or receive the occasional thank you call on a sobriety birthday. It requires faith on our part to keep trying.

_____

_____

_____

_____

_____

_____

_____

_____

_____

_____

_____

_____

June 16 — Reality

"I once heard a sober alcoholic say that drinking never made him happy, but it made him feel like he was going to be happy in about fifteen minutes. That was exactly it, and I couldn't understand why the happiness never came, couldn't see the flaw in my thinking, couldn't see that alcohol kept me trapped in a world of illusion, procrastination, paralysis. I lived always in the future, never in the present. Next time, next time! Next time I drank it would be different, next time it would make me feel good again. And all my efforts were doomed, because already drinking hadn't made me feel good in years."

Heather King, Parched

Many of us have been searching for happiness, or relief from misery, most of our lives. Drinking and drugging didn't do it; gambling or porn didn't do it; chaotic relationships didn't do it. Your only power is in staying in reality, seeing yourself clearly, and then making different choices.

_____

_____

_____

_____

_____

_____

_____

_____

_____

_____

_____

_____

June 17 — Motivation

"Why should you continue going after your dreams? Because seeing the look on the faces of the people who said you couldn't... will be priceless."

Kevin Ngo

Sometimes a strong sense of vindication can give someone energy to accomplish goals they were told they would never be able to do. I have had clients decide to stay sober to prove a point, and students go to school to prove they were smart enough. Does it really matter why someone enters recovery? What matters is the mindset we choose in order to stay clean sober, and eventually we need more motivation than proving a point. Motivational interviewing can be invaluable at this juncture. We can help our clients figure out a value-based motivation that will sustain them over time. What's your motivation in your work today?

_____
_____
_____
_____
_____
_____
_____
_____
_____
_____
_____
_____
_____

"If you want to be Awesome, You have to kick all the negative and boring people out of your life and arm yourself with awesomeness imbued with positivity, creativity and little bit of craziness."

Raideen Sarkar

This sounds like a bunch of recovering folks to me! People in recovery tend to think a little differently, tend to find weird things funny, and are incredibly resourceful. Working in treatment is rarely boring – we have no trouble getting all of our crisis intervention hours as interns! Recovering people are often able to retain their quirkiness in recovery, only better because we think more clearly and make better choices. We give up the self-destructive parts of our lifestyle and retain our creativity and resourcefulness. We can encourage our clients that life doesn't end in sobriety by being interesting ourselves!

_____

_____

_____

_____

_____

_____

_____

_____

_____

_____

_____

_____

_____

"Sometimes it is best to stand back from conflict and allow other elements in someone's life to do the hard work for you."

> *Bryant McGill, Simple Reminders: Inspiration for Living Your Best Life*

This is a great reminder that we are part of the process, but only a part. We can provide input, but research shows that the therapeutic relationship is 30% responsible for client change, while outside events have a 40% impact! What we do matters, but sometimes picking up a criminal case or losing a job can create an awakening even the best counselor could not initiate. Sometimes an agreement to stay married or retain parental rights can be more motivating than anything we do. Our job is to help our clients make the most of the events in their lives to support their ongoing recovery. Never underestimate the power of that contribution.

_____

_____

_____

_____

_____

_____

_____

_____

_____

_____

_____

_____

June 20 — FAMILY INVOLVEMENT

"You are evidence of your mother's strength, especially if you are a rebellious knucklehead and regardless she has always maintained her sanity."

Criss Jami

Family can be an integral part of ongoing recovery. Statistic back this up – people have a better chance at ongoing sobriety if they still have family support. This isn't easy because family can become afraid to hope, afraid to invest in the addict's recovery and then get hurt when they relapse. However, the family bond can be incredibly strong and can survive multiple disappointments. When the family begins to see their part of the addiction pattern and chooses to heal through therapy or Al-anon the whole family experiences the benefits of recovery. Some of us introduced our family to recovery through our own addiction process. Treatment works, and some of us are living proof!

_____

_____

_____

_____

_____

_____

_____

_____

_____

_____

_____

_____

"People who seek psychotherapy for psychological, behavioral or relationship problems tend to experience a wide range of bodily complaints...The body can express emotional issues a person may have difficulty processing consciously...I believe that the vast majority of people don't recognize what their bodies are really telling them. The way I see it, our emotions are music and our bodies are instruments that play the discordant tunes. But if we don't know how to read music, we just think the instrument is defective."

Charlette Mikulka

The stress of untreated codependency depletes our adrenal system and lowers our immune system. When we are disconnected from our bodies we lose track of the wisdom our bodies offer us. It tells us when we need to rest, eat, or foods to avoid because they leave s feeling heavy and sluggish afterwards. Encouraging our clients to inhabit their bodies is crucial.

_____

_____

_____

_____

_____

_____

_____

_____

_____

_____

_____

_____

JUNE 22 — CLARITY

"Be like water making its way through cracks. Do not be assertive, but adjust to the object, and you shall find a way round or through it. If nothing within you stays rigid, outward things will disclose themselves. Empty your mind, be formless. Shapeless, like water. If you put water into a cup, it becomes the cup. You put water into a bottle and it becomes the bottle. You put it in a teapot it becomes the teapot. Now, water can flow or it can crash. Be water my friend.

Bruce Lee

Entering every session with a clear mind allows us to enter the client's realty and see the world through their eyes. This is the definition of empathy. We need to empty our minds from preconceived notions about our clients and let them surprise us with unexpected wisdom or flashes of insight. This can be hard to do when clients appear to be shut down What if we were quiet – let the session unfold? When we're working harder than the client on their recovery something is wrong.

JUNE 23 — RESILIENCE

"The life of man is like a game with dice; if you don't get the throw you want, you must show your skill in making the best of the throw you get."

Terence

Some of us were dealt pretty hard hands in our lives. Trauma, mental illness, loss, addiction . . . all of these can be hard to survive. Yet survive we did. We've done more than survive – we're thriving. We're growing in our recovery and sharing what we've learned with those who still suffer every day. Our clients have survived similar trials and hardship, and they're with us instead of in the morgue. It's a part of our job to help them see that there might be some purpose in this, something they still have left to contribute that requires their presence.

"Are you all right, Sir?" asked Hezekiah.

"Just fighting over old battles in my mind," said John. *"It's the problem with age. You have all these rusty arguments, and no quarrel to use them in. My brain is a museum, but alas, I'm the only visitor, and even I am not terribly interested in the displays."*

Orson Scott Card, *Heartfire*

What kind of old arguments, old tapes, and well-nursed resentments are housed in your museum? We can so easily get lost in the past, ruminating and regretting. Often we're the only ones who remember the long-forgotten conversation, the moment of embarrassment, or bad decision. Reviewing the past can keep us sick, keep us trapped in our addiction and self-sabotage. Recovery gives us an option to focus on the future and create new memories. As counselors, we are able to help guide clients out of the maze of the past and into healthy options.

June 25 — Compromise

"The achievement of maturity, psychologically speaking, might be said to be the realization and acceptance that we simply cannot live independently from the world, and so we must live within it, with whatever compromises that might entail."

Paul Murray, Skippy Dies

What kind of compromises are you willing to make to develop healthy relationships with your friends and coworkers? In our addiction we seldom compromised, and relationships were more easily disposed of. After all, they were using acquaintances, not friendships. When we were using, we usually avoided those closest to us, preferring to isolate and use "in peace." Recovery programs emphasize unity and "principles above personalities" which gives us a roadmap to compromise and co-exist. We can learn to begin a conflict with our preferred ending in mind, which is often relationship preservation. This guides the words we choose and attitude we take in conversations.

"On a second note, though, I have something to say about pain. There are lots of kinds of pain. Pain of smashing your fingers in a car door, pains of losing a baby, pain of failing a test. But in their own little ways, these pains are all agonizing. Which is sad, and yet, happy, if you really think about it. If we never lost our car keys, or stepped in gum, or had a bad hair day, what kind of people would we be? In a word? Boring. We wouldn't be passionate; we wouldn't know it was exciting to get pregnant, or score an A on a final. So that's why, today at least, I am grateful for pain. Because it's part of what makes me the whacky, goofy, jaded, person that I am. Peace."

Alysha Speer

It's hard to be "grateful" for the perspective that pain and surviving pain can give us. Yet most of us would never change without it! Still we avoid it. What if we embraced it?

_____

_____

_____

_____

_____

_____

_____

_____

_____

_____

_____

_____

_____

"Sometimes I feel like I don't belong anywhere, & it's gonna take so long for me to get to somewhere,
Sometimes I feel so heavy hearted, but I can't explain cuz I'm so guarded. But that's a lonely road to travel, and a heavy load to bear. And it's a long, long way to heaven but I gotta get there
Can you send an angel?
Can you send me an angel...to guide me.

Alicia Keys

Is it possible that there is someone on your caseload right now who needs an angel? Our clients are lost, guarded, and their hearts are very heavy. Maybe you can remember a time when you were just as lonely and lost, and your empathy for the isolation they are feeling may create a bridge allowing you to meet. Every client that comes through our door has arrived with a purpose. It's not an accident that this client is on your caseload right now. Maybe they're here for you, as well? You never know when YOU will need an angel.

_____

_____

_____

_____

_____

_____

_____

_____

_____

_____

"The Christopher Columbus Award: This award goes to those who, like good old Chris, when they set out to do something, don't know where they are going; neither do they know how to get there. When they arrive, they don't know where they are, and when they return, they don't know where they've been."

Jim Berg, Changed Into His Image: God's Plan for Transforming Your Life

This made me smile! I have definitely earned the Christopher Columbus award on more than one occasion from time to time, aimlessly taking whatever was in front of me and winding up some place I never sought to be. This is a great description of addiction, actually and part of the challenge of counseling is to assist our clients to develop a plan for their recovery. Many of us were never taught decision-making skills so are difficulty being successful even when we do have a goal. This can be discouraging and supporting clients to have realistic hope when planning is an important part of our job.

_____

_____

_____

_____

_____

_____

_____

_____

_____

_____

"Some people are farsighted and some people are nearsighted. In the mind and in the heart. A farsighted person forgets your magic the closer that you get to them; the nearsighted person sees your magic more and more, the closer and closer that you become to them. You've got to find the nearsighted people. That's just a rule in life. And you've got to be one, too."

C. Joy Bell

This is a beautiful analogy, and a great reminder of our role in the life of our clients. We need to be nearsighted because it is very possible they have surrounded themselves with farsighted people for many, many years. But it's hard to see the magic in other people when you don't have people in your own life that are nearsighted. Do you see your own gifts, your own magic? It will help you to recognize the magic in others.

"Good men don't become legends," he said quietly.
"Good men don't need to become legends." She opened
her eyes, looking up at him. "They just do what's right any-
way."

Brandon Sanderson, The Well of Ascension

Integrity is hard to develop when you have spent
your life hiding. So, when some of us are finally living
a solid life we may want recognition for the changes
we have made. We see this in our clients when thy
have achieved a couple of weeks of sobriety and are
anxious that those around them see the difference in
them. They can be wounded on family day when their
family still seems distrustful or wary. We can prepare
clients that it may take a long time of steady, sober
behavior for the family to loosen their guard and stop
sniffing them every time they give them a hug.

_____
_____
_____
_____
_____
_____
_____
_____
_____
_____
_____
_____
_____

July 1 — Listening

"Talking is great, but don't ignore the value of listening. Pay attention to the words being spoken. Some people just love the sound of their own voice. And, when another person speaks, they are only anticipating to compete, challenge, or question what is being said. You can miss out on some important wisdom always running your mouth."

Amaka Imani Nkosazana

Bill W. warned against "Big shotism" for alcoholics. Some of us feel a need to weigh in with our opinions whether asked or not. Maybe we were never heard as children, maybe we're afraid of being overlooked or forgotten so we need to make our presence known! Counseling is a listening job- listening for what is unsaid as well as said. When you find yourself talking too much during psychoeducation group or therapy, maybe you need to be heard in your personal life. Sometimes it needs to be our turn to talk and be heard.

_____

_____

_____

_____

_____

_____

_____

_____

_____

_____

_____

_____

_____

"Who knows? Life may just be a Positive Conspiracy bent on putting us in the right place at the right time every living, breathing moment of the day. It just takes a certain kind of perspective to see this. Realizing this can put our "analyzer" on hold, our interpretive mind on "ga-ga" and our hearts on breathless."

Antero Alli, Angel Tech: A Modern Shaman's Guide to Reality Selection

This reminds me of the sponsor reminder that "we are right where we are supposed to be." This can be hard to swallow when we've just been dumped or are afraid our agency funding may be threatened. Our clients are in the right place with us at the right time. With the perspective of time they may come to realize this, even if they were mandated to participate. Sometimes we get glimpses of an outside force that seems to bring people together in perfect timing. It takes faith to see the wisdom in this when we are faced with painful circumstances.

"I value ethical standards, of course. But in a culture like ours – which devalues or dismisses the reality and power of the inner life – ethics too often becomes an external code of conduct, an objective set of rules we are told to follow, a moral exoskeleton we put on hoping to prop ourselves up. The problem with exoskeletons is simple: we can slip them off as easily as we can don them."

Parker J. Palmer

As counselors we can operate from mandatory ethics, which means the ethical standards we need to follow to not lose our license. We can also operate from aspirational ethics, which is a higher standard. It implies making ethical decision not just based on rules, which is the exoskeleton, but being guided by our higher self. Sometimes we set our sights on a standard created by someone we admire, 'What would my sponsor do?" or "What would Jesus do?" Ultimately ethics come from being an ethical person, not just a rule follower.

_____

_____

_____

_____

_____

_____

_____

_____

_____

_____

July 4 — Taking a risk

"For to be free is not merely to cast off one's chains, but to live in a way that respects and enhances the freedom of others."

Nelson Mandela

This is a man who knows something about the value of freedom! We've been transformed in our own recovery – we're different people with new skills and an emotional availability that was never possible in our addiction. Assisting our clients to access their own unique set of strengths and competences is a privilege. It's also a joy when we see them take risks that they would not be able or willing to take without support. When we demonstrate respect for clients we are modeling what self-respect might look like.

_____
_____
_____
_____
_____
_____
_____
_____
_____
_____
_____
_____
_____
_____
_____
_____
_____
_____

July 5 — Wounded healers

"Counselors are people who can utilize the traits of wisdom gained from their critical life experiences to help others. They are insightful, have the courage to recognize the suffering of the heart, and can relate to others through their own woundedness. They become a source of life and hope for others."

Linda C. Osterlund

Wounded healer is a term created by psychologist Carl Jung. The idea states that an analyst is compelled to treat patients because the analyst himself is "wounded." It's true that many of us DO feel compelled to give back what we've been freely given. It's exciting and healing to take the worst of our lives and transform it into a source of healing for others. It gives purpose to our suffering, and I've been grateful more than once so see wisdom I gained the hard way comfort someone else.

"We can either watch life from the sidelines, or actively participate...Either we let self-doubt and feelings of inadequacy prevent us from realizing our potential, or embrace the fact that when we turn our attention away from ourselves, our potential is limitless."

Christopher Reeve

Many of us, and our clients, survived our childhood by assuming a lost child role. We assisted people we love by being self-sufficient and not asking for what we need and want. We are comfortable in our company, and have lived our lives as observers. While we observe every nuance and expression, we rarely participate in the discussion. It seems too risky to be so visible and run the risk of being a "problem." As counselors we are called to participate and invite observer clients to enter the process. This is easier to do if we're fully participating in our own lives and not watching from the sidelines. How fully involved are you in your life?

_____

_____

_____

_____

_____

_____

_____

_____

_____

_____

*"I paid, got up, walked
to the door, opened it.*

*I heard the man
say, "that guy's
nuts."*

*Out on the street I
walked north
feeling
curiously
honored."*

Charles Bukowski

People in recovery frequently think "outside the box" and there are times when people may respond with a "huh?" That's why being with other recovering people can be so comforting. We can refer to situations in our lives, our reactive responses and know we will be heard without judgment. Most often, we are heard with a smile and nod of recognition!

_____

_____

_____

_____

_____

_____

_____

_____

_____

_____

_____

JULY 8 — CHANGING RELATIONSHIPS

"DETOX your mind, body, AND your contact list."

SupaNova Slom, The Remedy

Changing our relationships with others is crucial in long-term recovery. More often than not our clients believe that they can maintain their relationships and lifestyle after rehab without changes. I'm sure you've experienced clients who plan to go to the bar to test their new recovery and just listen to the music. Sometimes they even plan to be the designated driver! Watching them vastly underestimating the power of the disease of addiction is scary. However, even with long-term recovery helpers may still have areas in their life they are overestimating their "control" over. How about you? Is there an area you need to surrender in your recovery?

_____

_____

_____

_____

_____

_____

_____

_____

_____

_____

_____

_____

_____

_____

July 9 — Enjoying our own company

"The key is the ability, whether innate or conditioned, to find the other side of the rote, the picayune, the meaningless, the repetitive, the pointlessly complex. To be, in a word, unborable … If you are immune to boredom, there is literally nothing you cannot accomplish."

David Foster Wallace, The Pale King

Clients often cite boredom as a reason for relapse or using. In our addiction our words become so small, our internal landscape so barren, that when we are alone no one's home! We are always looking outside of ourselves for stimulation, not realizing our internal world can be a source of growth and interest. Recovery requires us to develop our internal world, take personal inventories, and become more aware of what we bring to the table. A relationship with ourselves is the best long-term relationship we will ever have! Are you entertained in your own company?

_____

_____

_____

_____

_____

_____

_____

_____

_____

_____

_____

_____

July 10 — Influencing Others

"Sometimes the slightest things change the directions of our lives, the merest breath of a circumstance, a random moment that connects like a meteorite striking the earth. Lives have swiveled and changed direction on the strength of a chance remark."

Bryce Courtenay

One of the challenges for new counselors is to recognize that our words now have power. Clients assume that our comments are accurate and that we can see something in them they may not see of themselves. So when we're sarcastic or flip we can make a chance comment that we immediately forget, but that stays with a client. Maybe we joked about their assignment or teases them about their using history. As a counselor our words need to be carefully chosen with intention to be effective. We need to be mindful of our comments, which is not a bad thing to practice outside of work as well!

_____

_____

_____

_____

_____

_____

_____

_____

_____

_____

_____

_____

July 11 — Meaning in our work

"The most emotionally demanding aspect of a work situation is its lack of existential significance. People need meaning in their lives, and the failure to find such meaning will cause burnout. It is not objective failure per se that causes burnout but rather the feeling that one's efforts are insignificant and meaningless. Similarly, it is not objective success per se that prevents burnout but rather subjective experience of doing something meaningful."

Wilmar B Schaufeli, Christina Maslach and Tadeusz Marek

Do you find meaning in your work in recovery? In Positive Psychology they make the point that we need to have a combination of meaning and pleasure for greatest life happiness. Our work is challenging at times, and the paperwork and chaos can begin to strip the pleasure from our job. It's important to make the time to do your favorite part of your job, most often interacting with clients in a meaningful way.

_____

_____

_____

_____

_____

_____

_____

_____

_____

_____

_____

_____

"He becomes angry, indignant, self-pitying. What is his basic trouble? Is he not really a self-seeker even when trying to be kind? Is he not a victim of the delusion that he can wrest satisfaction and happiness out of this world if he only manages well?"

AA, 2001, p. 161

What a great reminder of the fallacy of control! We honestly begin to believe that if we just controlled a situation more effectively all would be well! The more we try to control the more irritable and discontent we become. Clients spending their time on the phone managing their families often hang up frustrated and angry. We can help clients recognize the feelings attached to futile attempts to control, and help them connect with this the powerlessness of using. We can remember our own moments or powerlessness to keep us empathetic.

_____

_____

_____

_____

_____

_____

_____

_____

_____

_____

_____

_____

"I have found it of enormous value when I can permit myself to understand the other person. The way in which I have worded in this statement may seem strange to you. Is it necessary to permit oneself to understand another? I think that it is. Our first reaction to most of the statements which we hear from other people is an evaluation, or judgment, rather than an understanding of it. When someone expresses some feeling or attitude or belief, our tendency is, almost immediately, to feel That's right; or That's stupid; That's abnormal; That's unreasonable; That's incorrect; That's not nice. Very rarely do we permit ourselves to understand precisely what the meaning of the statement is to the other person."

Carl Rogers

Entering someone's world and seeing the world through their eyes is a tremendous sign of respect.

_____

_____

_____

_____

_____

_____

_____

_____

_____

_____

_____

_____

_____

_____

"Some luck lies in not getting what you thought you wanted but getting what you have, which once you have got it you may be smart enough to see is what you would have wanted had you known."

Garrison Keillor

When we are loaded, coming home at 7:00 am when everyone else is heading to work, we're watching them through a window. Their lives seem so foreign because our lives are lived upside down. We can't imagine WANTING to have somewhere to go at 7:00 am.! However, sobriety teaches us to value being a participant in the world, being a contributor gives us a place at the table. Our self-esteem increases, and we can come out of the shadows. We have the wisdom to appreciate where we've come. Maybe we'll even have gratitude.

JULY 15 — FLOW IN WORK

"Ah? A small aversion to menial labor?" The doctor cocked an eyebrow. "Understandable, but misplaced. One should treasure those hum-drum tasks that keep the body occupied but leave the mind and heart unfettered."

Tad Williams, The Dragonbone Chair

In positive psychology, Flow, also known as Zone, is the mental state of operation in which a person performing an activity is fully immersed in a feeling of energized focus, full involvement, and enjoyment in the process of the activity. In essence, flow is characterized by complete absorption in what one does. There are moments when we're leading a group and time seems disappears. This can also happen when we're absorbed in a hobby that delights and challenges us. I have a dear friend that swears this is her experience when she irons! I know other people who talk about this when the garden. When do you find your flow?

_____

_____

_____

_____

_____

_____

_____

_____

_____

_____

_____

_____

July 16 — Self-Compassion

"Jesus tells us: 'Love your neighbor as yourself' (Mk 12:31). How can we love our neighbor if we can't or won't love ourselves, at least a little? When we hold ourselves to unrealistic standards, that perfectionist attitude can't help but trickle down. It becomes harder to have compassion for others if we have no compassion for ourselves."

Mary DeTurris Poust, Cravings: A Catholic Wrestles with Food, Self-Image, and God

How are you doing with your expectations for yourself? Are your expectations reasonable? Do you value your humanity or see it as a problem to fix? Love and compassion do start with our internal experience of our value. It is hard to extend forgiveness and compassion to others when we don't know what it feels like. It is not true that we have different standards for others than we do for ourselves. If we're honest with ourselves, we silently judge them when they fail as hard as we judge ourselves.

_____

_____

_____

_____

_____

_____

_____

_____

_____

_____

_____

_____

"There is a yearning that is as spiritual as it is sensual. Even when it degenerates into addiction, there is something salvageable from the original impulse that can only be described as sacred. Something in the person (dare we call it a soul?) wants to be free, and it seeks its freedom any way it can. ... There is a drive for transcendence that is implicit in even the most sensual of desires."

Mark Epstein, Open to Desire: Embracing a Lust for Life - Insights from Buddhism and Psychotherapy

Carl Jung drew the connection with alcohol as a spirit, and people have been attempting to explore the spiritual word with the aid of substances from the beginning of time. When we leave ourselves through meditation, we enter this other realm as our boundaries blur into the people and the spiritual world. And we don't need ecstasy or ketamine.

July 18 — Using time

Laugh when you can,
apologize when you should,
and let go of what you can't change.
Life's too short to be anything... but happy.

Anonymous

What an interesting version of the Serenity Prayer! Laughter can't be overemphasized if we want to stay sane and sober. This means our side of the street needs to be clean and we're working a daily 10th Step to own out part of the problem. When we own it we can address whatever it is and put it behind us. Many of us never thought we would live past 30, sometimes 21. Our lives were pretty reckless, and we never planned for a future. Yet here we are! Having lost our lives for many years, our time in recovery seems even more precious. Are you spending the time you have left the way you want to spend it?

_____

_____

_____

_____

_____

_____

_____

_____

_____

_____

_____

_____

July 19 — Compassion

"It's common to reject or punish yourself when you've been rejected by others. When you experience disappointment from the way your family or others treat you, that's the time to take special care of yourself. What are you doing to nurture yourself? What are you doing to protect yourself? Find a healthy way to express your pain."

Christina Enevoldsen

Even when clients enter recovery it is possible the family is not acknowledging the effects of addiction on the family system. So, it's possible that they will continue to react to the client in recovery very similarly to when they were using. This can be frustrating and discouraging to say the least. It's our job to begin to treat the client as a member of the recovering community. This means to treat them with dignity and respect, and give them the benefit of the doubt when possible. We need to keep our cynicism at bay!

_____

_____

_____

_____

_____

_____

_____

_____

_____

_____

_____

_____

"We have this attitude that people become drug addicts against their will. That they couldn't possibly want this kind of life. But maybe that's not true. Maybe they don't want to live like other people — it just wouldn't suit them."

Jo Nesbø

This is an interesting thought. If we put aside the disease model for a moment, it's worth considering. Many of our clients would be candidates for the "island of misfit toys." They are somewhat socially awkward, have narrow interests, and are often stimulant seeking so have a high tolerance for stress. When they think about sitting in a cubicle in front of a computer, or think about wearing pantyhose, they simply can't bear the thought. They are also alternative learners, like many of us, which makes us the ideal support!

_____

_____

_____

_____

_____

_____

_____

_____

_____

_____

_____

_____

_____

_____

July 21 — Amends

"The goal was never dependent on the route that took me there. It was always dependent on the heart that got me through whatever route opened itself up to my efforts."

Dan Pearce, Single Dad Laughing

Our road to recovery is frequently filled with unexpected twists and turns, and it requires amazing amounts of faith to keep moving forward. It takes faith to trust that the roadblocks are ultimately in our best interest, and to surrender the outcome. The Twelve Steps provides a roadmap to monitor our motives, and to take regular inventories where we're honest with ourselves about our impact on others. If you need to make an amends you've been avoiding, maybe today is a good day to clean your side of the street.

_____

_____

_____

_____

_____

_____

_____

_____

_____

_____

_____

_____

_____

_____

_____

"Public truth telling is a form of recovery, especially when combined with social action. Sharing traumatic experiences with others enables victims to reconstruct repressed memory, mourn loss, and master helplessness, which is trauma's essential insult. And, by facilitating reconnection to ordinary life, the public testimony helps survivors restore basic trust in a just world and overcome feelings of isolation. But the talking cure is predicated on the existence of a community willing to bear witness. 'Recovery can take place only within the context of relationships,' write Judith Herman. 'It cannot occur in isolation."

Lawrence N. Powell, Troubled Memory: Anne Levy, the Holocaust, and David Duke's Louisiana

Truth and service can be a powerful combination. Having others bear witness to our lives is healing.

_____

_____

_____

_____

_____

_____

_____

_____

_____

_____

_____

_____

_____

_____

_____

July 23 — Integrity

"In a world filled with flaky people, those that honor commitments and do what they say STAND-OUT. Integrity is currency."

Matthew Loop

Have you found this to be true? Integrity is a big deal in recovery. When we're out their running amok integrity is one of the first qualities we're willing to sacrifice! Being accountable, even in small things, takes a long time in recovery. It's important to remember that our clients will find it easier to get clean than be honest, and it will help to remember how much longer our honesty took than our sobriety! I was driving to a meeting with a friend once who had 5 years, and his phone rang. I heard him say, "We're in Target." I was shocked, and when he hung up he said, "I'm not sure why I said that." Integrity takes some of us longer than others.

"Before speaking, consult your inner-truth barometer, and resist the temptation to tell people only what they want to hear."

Wayne W. Dyer

This can be easier said than done. Some of us have been people-pleasers since childhood, a strategy designed to keep our relationships with other people stable. It takes a lot of courage to risk honesty with people who matter to us. This includes clients, who need us to point out what we see, cushioned by genuine compassion and respect. Being honest with someone is a high form of respect, and when we see client's dong old behavior or running a game we need to let them know we SEE them. We owe them this.

"It is not kindness to tell patients that need strong medicine that nothing serious is wrong with them."

Cornelius Van Til

July 25 — Mirrors

"People are going to come into your life, and God is going to use them to help you. To them you're insignificant and don't matter. They are not going to understand you, or even see the point of why God had you hang in there with them for so long. Remember this: Sometimes meeting someone has nothing to do with what you can provide for him or her and everything to do with what God needs you to recognize in that person. If you didn't understand the message, God will keep sending the same person or situation into your life."

Shannon L. Alder

We never know why someone has entered our lives. In our role as a helper we may assume we are there for the client, but it's possible that they have something to teach us about us that will be priceless. Pay attention to strong reactions to clients – maybe they're a mirror!

_____

_____

_____

_____

_____

_____

_____

_____

_____

_____

_____

"Every plan in which we participate has one constant, ourselves. Not that we are always the same, but that we are always part of the plan. All else comes and goes: friends, parents, possessions, conditions, situations, and associates, leaving only us, ourselves."

> Wu Wei, I Ching Wisdom: More Guidance from the
> Book of Answers, Volume Two

It's important to remember that we are the common denominator in all of the situations in our lives. It's helpful to look for patterns when we start to feel victimized. I know you've met with clients who describe conflict patterns with others that seem to repeat in work settings, home settings, and friendships. They seem oblivious that they are the recurring factor! As an outsider we can see the larger picture and draw compassionate attention to what we see. Recognizing this pattern is their hope for change.

"Imagine yourself near the end of your life. You are relaxing in a rocking chair reflecting on the decision you presently want to make. As the older, wiser you thinks about the outcome of your choice, ask yourself three simple questions.
1. Did it cause harm?
2. Did it bring about good?
3. How did it shape the person I became?
The Rocking Chair Test helps you to take a long view of your options. After imagining your answers to those questions, you should know better which way to go."

Steve Goodier

Keeping the end of our life in mind is helpful in making our decisions today. In Al-anon we ask, "How important is it?" which allows us to be . responsive instead of reactive in making our choices. The choices we make now do shape the person we will become.

_____

_____

_____

_____

_____

_____

_____

_____

_____

_____

_____

_____

_____

_____

JULY 28 — SELF-COMPASSION

"And once we have the condition of peace and joy in us, we can afford to be in any situation. Even in the situation of hell, we will be able to contribute our peace and serenity. The most important thing is for each of us to have some freedom in our heart, some stability in our heart, some peace in our heart. Only then will we be able to relieve the suffering around us."

> Thich Nhat Hanh, Vietnamese Buddhist teacher,
> interviewed by Ram Dass, as quoted in
> *Inquiring Mind Magazine*, Spring 1996 issue

We're reminded that alleviating the suffering around us starts with addressing our own suffering. Even in sobriety we may still be suffering from depression, anxiety, or PTSD. Some people in recovery believe we should "Don't take nothing never." So, we avoid the psychiatric medications we need that would increase the quality of our life. It's important that this be resolved for you to be an advocate for your clients. Err on the side of compassion.

JULY 29 — FOOTWORK

"Don't ask for directions if you're not going to start the car."

Rob Liano

I love this! Some of us suffer from "analyses paralysis." We gather evidence, check websites, and solicit option after option . . . and we don't pull the trigger. Fear of being wrong can be powerfully limiting. Most of the decisions we will make in life can be undone. Sometime with effort and inconvenience, but life offer many "do-overs." Some of us were shamed when we made mistakes, and still carry our inner-critic that sits on the sidelines and harshly evaluates every decision we consider. It's time to fire this member of our inner committee. "No" is not always the right answer. Life is too short to constantly wait for the perfect situation or circumstance to appear.

_____

_____

_____

_____

_____

_____

_____

_____

_____

_____

_____

_____

_____

_____

July 30 — Changing our patterns

"Don't let a thief into your house three times. The first time was enough. The second time was a chance. The third time means you're stupid."

C. JoyBell C.

What's OUR role in the disastrous relationships in our life? Yes, our picker was broken and we may have invited people in our lives that used us, took advantage of us, and cheated on us. However, we may have taken them back over and over again, each time hoping for a different outcome. It's not about blame, it's about using the power we have to look at our part of the pattern and shift our responses to the people in our lives. Choosing badly may have left us feeling defeated and hopeless. Seeing our part can give us realistic hope for change. This is an important message to pass on to our clients who have left lots of thieves into their house and need to change this to stay sober.

_____

_____

_____

_____

_____

_____

_____

_____

_____

_____

_____

_____

July 31 — Gratitude

"To improve quality of life, to evolve into a better version of ourselves, to pause in recognition of blessings with only our name on the tag, to dance in gratitude, to embrace with abandon, to give without receiving, to seek the face of God ... all this and more is why we exist."

Toni Sorenson

Life offers us such joy! We can get so caught up in the day to day obligations of life that seem to suck our time from us. Life is full of small irritants and inconveniences, and we can forget to keep this in perspective. That the frustrations are only part of the picture of our lives. We have the rewards of sobriety, and relationships we have established in our sobriety to rejoice in. We've created new lives full of opportunity for travel, education, and friendship. This perspective is important when we're faced with the discouragement of our clients who are mired in the consequences of their disease. It would be easy to get sucked into their energy.

_____

_____

_____

_____

_____

_____

_____

_____

_____

_____

_____

"There's an undeniable healing power in telling the truth to someone who validates you by simply listening . . . honor washes away the stench of shame."

Jo Ann Fore

New counselors can be worried that they're not saying enough or giving enough direction. They worry about "what to say," and "what questions to ask." Much of our time is spent listening. Listening with our full presence honors to the story our clients have to tell. So many of us have never really been heard. We rarely hear our own voice, and when someone is attentive for minutes at a time we can begin to hear ourselves. We hear our wisdom and hear our bullshit. We can reflect back the client what we hear and offer a new perspective. Most of us need a witness to our lives, which includes our friends, family and sponsor. We cannot heal in isolation.

"The word 'survivor' carries a weight of remembrance that has broken the minds and bodies of more than a few men and women. It also contains a humbling light of recognition that compels many to do whatever they can to help reinforce the efforts of those who might be 'at risk' of not just giving up on their dreams, but of giving up on their continued existence."

Aberjhani, Illuminated Corners: Collected Essays and Articles Volume I.

Many people who work in alcohol and drug treatment could describe themselves as survivors. Addiction is a hazardous lifestyle, and we have narrowly missed death on one or more occasion. Some of us attempted to end our lives, and are still here. There is something left for us to do, and we've chosen to assist others to heal as a way to heal ourselves, if we're honest. It works. Service IS healing, and every time a client heals we heal with them because healing energy is shared energy.

August 3 — Self-Acceptance

"Accept yourself. Love yourself as you are. Your finest work, your best movements, your joy, peace, and healing comes when you love yourself. You give a great gift to the world when you do that. You give others permission to do the same: to love themselves. Revel in self-love. Roll in it as you would sunshine."

Melodie Beattie

It may sound weird to hear that loving ourselves is a "gift to the world." It makes sense when you think about the energy we carry in the world and the way our energy can affect others. I know you've had the experience of being affected by someone who has a negative vibe – without realizing it your own mood can begin to shift. This can happen with a positive vibe as well. There are people in our life who seem to change the atmosphere in the room when they walk in. Things lighten, and you find yourself smiling despite yourself. Maybe this is you?

_____

_____

_____

_____

_____

_____

_____

_____

_____

_____

_____

"And yet many of us do it without families," Nynaeve said. "Without love, without passion beyond our own particular interests. So even while we try to guide the world, we separate ourselves from it. We risk arrogance, Egwene. We always assume we know best, but risk making ourselves unable to fathom the people we claim to serve."

Robert Jordan

It's is possible for helpers with a lot of clean time to feel distanced from clients in early recovery. Without knowing it, we may take on a superior attitude, or be impatient with the drama and chaos of early recovery in residential treatment. We may forget our own early years in sobriety, and may have forgotten how stressed out and emotionally raw we were. During that time, it took people who were patient and available to provide the stability we needed to retain our recovery progress. Remember that, "There but for the grace of God go I."

_____

_____

_____

_____

_____

_____

_____

_____

_____

_____

_____

_____

August 5 — Self-Care

"Don't sacrifice yourself too much, because if you sacrifice too much there's nothing else you can give and nobody will care for you."

Karl Lagerfeld

It is impossible to draw from an empty well. We become empty when we don't have balance in our lives. We work too many extra shifts, take on too many classes, manage too much drama in or personal life. Over time our adrenal system begins to poop out and our patience and emotional availability for our clients and co-workers is stretched too thin. We snap, are sarcastic, and avoid returning phone calls that could be crucial for case management. It's wise to know when it's time to take a mental health day, or maybe even a week away. The treatment center will function quite well, even better maybe, if you've become hard to work with!

_____

_____

_____

_____

_____

_____

_____

_____

_____

_____

_____

_____

"The most radical and far-reaching solutions often need rethinking of processes and deep questioning of the status quo-and these are hard."

Bill Price, The Best Service is No Service

New innovations in recovery treatment are being developed all the time. When I was in graduate school in the 80's we still believed that brain cells died in alcoholism and once lost would not be replaced. We now know about brain plasticity and the prognosis for brain healing is so much better than we knew! We now have Motivational Interviewing instead of "breaking denial," and interventions are now far more systems aware and invitational. Acknowledging the trauma of the addiction lifestyle through Trauma-informed treatment has been introduce into mainstream treatment, and our toolbox is larger than ever. These innovations took questioning traditional methods, and treatment has never been more effective. What status quo do you need to challenge today?

_____

_____

_____

_____

_____

_____

_____

_____

_____

_____

"I never expect appreciation. I always set a deadline for the things I have to do to be a successful person, when I complete them, I give myself a piece of candy, a glass of tea and some free time to enjoy- that is how I honor my hardworking and appreciate my struggles."

M.F. Moonzajer, LOVE, HATRED AND MADNESS

How much of a cheerleader are you for yourself? Daily living requires a certain amount of thankless self-discipline. We go to work when we don't "feel" like it – a major change from our using days! Daily life, including bill paying, laundry, bathroom cleaning, and hygiene don't offer us an audience. Even when people live with us they may not recognize our contribution and clap when we take out the trash! So, we need to appreciate ourselves and take a few minutes to recognize and acknowledge our efforts to make our lives successful on a daily basis. Success is in the details.

"Prayer is not as complex as it may seem. When we are at a loss for words, sometimes the simplest thing to do is make a mental list of all the good things in our lives (family, friends, pets, etc.) and with a grateful heart just say... "Thank you God"."

Tom Hackett

Prayer and meditation is an important part of a program for Twelve Step members. However, gratitude can be a sufficient prayer even for those who still struggle with the Third Step Power because it doesn't require us to define the Higher Power. It's also a good practice for people in early recovery. The gratitude list will grow with time in sobriety if they make this part of their daily ritual. How about you? Are you offering prayers of gratitude for your life or your chance to work with others still suffering in the disease? The opportunity to use our checkered past to help others is a miracle.

_____

_____

_____

_____

_____

_____

_____

_____

_____

_____

_____

"It doesn't matter how many say it cannot be done or how many people have tried it before; it's important to realize that whatever you're doing, it's your first attempt at it."
Wally Amos

Comparing ourselves to others is a slippery slope of shame and discouragement. Many of us don't have a strong learning curve - we're impatient when we're fumbling around and still learning. One of the mistakes my student interns make is to compare themselves to people with 15 years' experience which then leads them to feel inadequate and unskilled. It's such an unfair comparison! I encourage them to be kind to themselves and recognize the skills they demonstrated on a daily basis at the treatment center. If you're learning something new right now I encourage you to be patient with yourself today.

_____
_____
_____
_____
_____
_____
_____
_____
_____
_____
_____
_____
_____
_____
_____

"A moment of truth is very powerful. Instead of smiling to be polite, just frown. Instead of laughing when you are nervous or uncomfortable, just speak your truth. Instead of acting like everything is all right, proclaim it isn't alright, and talk about your feelings! Honor your truth. Honor yourself. Be real."

Bryant McGill, Simple Reminders: Inspiration for Living Your Best Life

Do you remember the story of the Velveteen Rabbit?
"Generally, by the time you are Real, most of your hair has been loved off, and your eyes drop out and you get loose in the joints and very shabby. But these things don't matter at all, because once you are Real you can't be ugly, except to people who don't understand."

Margery Williams, The Velveteen Rabbit

When we're honest about our internal world we're giving the people in our lives a chance to love us. We may struggle with believing we're truly "loveable" so it's important that the people in our lives have a chance to demonstrate it on a regular basis.

"If you align the Serenity prayer onto the blueprint of the Medicine Wheel, the part that says to accept the things I cannot change falls at the South node. The South is the time period of the past. Therefore, the only thing you cannot change is in the past."

Renee Bledsoe

Do you believe this is true? When we find ourselves ruminating about the past it's a sign that we have not come to peace with our history. Maybe we need to make a formal amends, or maybe we need to forgive ourselves for the decisions we made in the past. In addiction, our decisions were a result of reactivity and cravings, and we did not have access to the frontal lobe decision making that's based on response and reflection. We offer a living amends every day we respond instead of react. Every time we use our history to help someone else we're shifting our karma debt. True forgiveness requires us to suspend judgment about ourselves.

_____

_____

_____

_____

_____

_____

_____

_____

_____

_____

_____

"A dwarf will fight for honor, but a man will kill for pride."
Auron thought for a moment. "What's the difference?"
"Honor is how others see you. Pride is how you see your-
self."

E.E. Knight, Dragon Champion

What an interesting thought! Pride can be really dis-
torting, and we are operating in what Anne Wilson
Schaef calls, "impression management." We spend
a lot of time attempting to control the image others
have of us, and this is usually driven by pride. Or
maybe something else. Maybe we worry about being
an "imposter." If people really knew who we were
they wouldn't hire us or trust us next to their purse!
Honor is earned by behaving honorably. This means
doing the next right thing on a regular basis, which
creates a level of trust and respect we could never
have "forced" with our image!

_____

_____

_____

_____

_____

_____

_____

_____

_____

_____

_____

_____

_____

"Allowing enthusiasm to bubble up from you and pervade your very existence will bring an abundance of joy to yourself and others. It's one of the simplest ways I can think of to serve others."

Carlson & Carlson, 2001, p. 163

People gravitate towards those who have passion and enthusiasm for their work. Your clients will recognize your genuine love for what you do, which can encourage them to invest in their own recovery. Remember that recovery is based on "attraction and not promotion" which happens when people in recovery demonstrate that recovery really works. Our clients are afraid that their lives are over – that life in sobriety will be grey, lack stimulation and challenge. When we have a genuine smile for the clients and they hear our laughter they can have hope!

_____
_____
_____
_____
_____
_____
_____
_____
_____
_____
_____
_____
_____
_____

"Be like a duck, paddling and working very hard inside the water, but what everyone sees is a smiling and calm face."

Manoj Arora, From the Rat Race to Financial Freedom

We are aware of the financial stressors of working in treatment. Management worries about shifts in the budget and census. Often, their worry is passed down to us, and we might even worry about our jobs. It can be hard to concentrate when this is happening, and yet we're required by professionalism to walk into groups with a calm focus. And we do! We compartmentalize our concerns and turn our attention to their concerns. It may even be a welcome respite from our worry to use our energy to meet the needs of the clients, and feel like we're being effective. Freedom from financial fear is one of the promises. We need to claim it!

_____

_____

_____

_____

_____

_____

_____

_____

_____

_____

_____

_____

_____

August 15 — Influencing others

"I have learned that real angels don't have gossamer white robes and Cherubic skin, they have calloused hands and smell of the days' sweat."

Richard Paul Evans, Lost December

When I picture the average staffing of a treatment center there are very few angels wings! There are tattoos, weathered faces, and very often we smell of smoke and coffee! We may look a little dog-eared, but the wisdom we carry is hard-won, and our weathered look may be a relief to the new addict in recovery. We look familiar, and this can be comforting. Working in treatment is hard work, and not for the lazy. We're moving almost all day, multi-tasking while listening to people, reassuring, checking with parole, leading groups, putting out crisis after crisis. And we volunteered for this job! We ARE angels even if we don't recognize it.

_____

_____

_____

_____

_____

_____

_____

_____

_____

_____

_____

_____

_____

"Sometimes nothing is the best thing to say and often the best thing to do."

> Michael Thomas Sunnarborg, *21 Steps to Better Relationships: Find More Balance with Others*

This is the hardest advice in the world for Codependents and helpers. We show love by having the answers and feel COMPELLED to say something when confronted by someone's anxiety. That really is the heart of the matter – we're triggered when someone is anxious around us. The more we love the, the greater the trigger! One of the most loving things we can do is to allow them to sort through their own thinking and decision making without imposing our opinion. Sitting still and simply listening, waiting to be ASKED for our input is the most professional and respectful position we can take.

_____

_____

_____

_____

_____

_____

_____

_____

_____

_____

_____

_____

"It's not the load that breaks you down, it's the way you carry it."

Lou Holtz

Some of us are still working our way through the wreckage we created in our addiction. Maybe we're still feeling the impact of a family member's addiction. Or, maybe we're still earning back custody of our children. Maybe we're addressing medical issues that developed when we were using or caretaking an alcoholic in our family. Despite this worry, we show up every day to work with people who are still struggling in their disease, and this isn't easy work. Carrying yourself with dignity and being part of the solution is the best role modeling possible. To maintain this, a support system is crucial. The people who care for you want to be part of your solution.

_____

_____

_____

_____

_____

_____

_____

_____

_____

_____

_____

_____

_____

"When we are no longer able to change a situation, we are challenged to change ourselves."

Viktor E. Frankl, Man's Search for Meaning

We can change three things in a situation: our behavior, our attitude, or the situation. Clients struggle with this on a regular basis. Perhaps they came it through an intervention or were mandated by the court. Mostly they fight the situation. We are able to remind them of the other options; change in attitude or behavior. This takes support, reminders, and an example. How well are you managing your life situation? Recovery teaches us that we can "act as if" and try new behavior, and also teaches us that feelings are not facts. We can start our day over at any point, and there is a lot freedom in this. Attitude is everything if we want to remain sane and sober.

_____

_____

_____

_____

_____

_____

_____

_____

_____

_____

_____

_____

_____

"People tend to be generous when sharing their nonsense, fear, and ignorance. And while they seem quite eager to feed you their negativity, please remember that sometimes the diet we need to be on is a spiritual and emotional one. Be cautious with what you feed your mind and soul. Fuel yourself with positivity and let that fuel propel you into positive action."

Steve Maraboli, Unapologetically You: Reflections on Life and the Human Experience

Who's in your life right now? In every family group we're faced with toxic, controlling, family members who may create stress for clients when they leave the treatment setting. They need help for themselves to address their broken hearts. Broken hearts can look angry, resentful, betrayed . . . and can trigger helpers with their own family issues. It's important for recovering people, including us, to be careful with the energy surrounding us. Maybe we should skip Criminal Minds before bed tonight!

August 20 — Motivation

"But one of the worst results of being a slave and being forced to do things is that when there is no one to force you any more you find you have almost lost the power of forcing yourself."

C.S. Lewis, The Horse and His Boy

If you've been working in the addiction field a long time you've seen clients do really well in recovery only to relapse when they finally discharge probation or regain custody. It seems so crazy until you realize that people will often program well when they have external control. If someone has been in the system since adolescence they may have very little ability to self-motivate. To stay clean they'll need to shift their motivation to an internal one. This is the power of Motivational Interviewing. We focus on the client's values and attempt to align their recovery goals accordingly. This is their best shot to make that shift in the long run.

_____

_____

_____

_____

_____

_____

_____

_____

_____

_____

_____

August 21 — Self-Compassion

"Where did we ever get the crazy idea that in order to make children do better, first we have to make them feel worse? Think of the last time you felt humiliated or treated unfairly. Did you feel like cooperating or doing better?"

Jane Nelsen

It's possible that you were motivated by parental criticism as a child. This can also be cultural, parents concerned about children not becoming complacent, but continuing to excel. The flaw with his theory is that failure becomes a result of character, and we can develop a shame-core. A natural response to shame is to deny mistakes, lie, and avoid risks. So many of our clients have experienced this in their early lives, and it helps to have compassion for shame when they bristle when we remind them of their chore or ask them to complete an assignment. Do you have this same tendency to bristle when your supervisor points our an error in your paperwork? These clients may be your mirror.

_____
_____
_____
_____
_____
_____
_____
_____
_____
_____
_____

"You don't go walking into the proverbial lion's den lightly. You start with a good breakfast."

Jim Butcher, Storm Front

Breakfast is my favorite meal, so I loved this quote. It's a great reminder of the importance of preparation physically as well as spiritually. Self-care is nutritional as well as emotional. I ask my clients, "Would you pack half a bagel, a thermos of coffee and a cigarette for your third grader and say, "Okay, see you this afternoon" as you drop them off? Of course not! But we give ourselves this diet on a regular basis. Or maybe we live at the drive through, and have mastered unwrapping a burger without dripping while driving! Treatment can feel like a lion's den sometimes as well never really know what we'll be met with when we enter the building. So much can change between shifts, and we never know what crisis will be waiting in our office. It helps to concentrate if you've had some protein and fiber.

"The death of a dream can in fact serve as the vehicle that endows it with new form, with reinvigorated substance, a fresh flow of ideas, and splendidly revitalized color. In short, the power of a certain kind of dream is such that death need not indicate finality at all but rather signify a metaphysical and metaphorical leap forward."

Aberjhani, The River of Winged Dreams

When my last relationship ended I thought my life was over. Sometimes when we quit using, we feel our life is over. At first the world feel black, white and grey. Slowly but surely color begins to peek out here and there, and we begin to suspect that we will survive the loss. The next thing we know we hear ourselves laugh unexpectedly and begin to picture a future. It's a revised future, maybe even better future than we would have ever imagined. As much as we fought the loss of our life as we knew it, it was ultimately liberating.

_____

_____

_____

_____

_____

_____

_____

_____

_____

_____

_____

_____

"I'd rather go into a competition as the underdog. Less pressure to perform, and more motivation."

Jarod Kintz, Seriously delirious, but not at all serious

This made me laugh! It's the path of least resistance, which for many of us is a well-worn path. Success can be really scary because we'll be expected to maintain the success. This is the real pressure. Many of us have no trouble working hard to put our lives together, staying focused and even clean and sober throughout the process. It's the success that throws us for a loop. We're not sure what to do with the good job, running vehicle, solid relationship. Most of our skills were developed to cope with chaos ad drama, so we feel a little lost when things settle down. It's important to identify this pattern for yourself because it leads to a lot of self-sabotage.

_____

_____

_____

_____

_____

_____

_____

_____

_____

_____

_____

_____

_____

"Yawns are not the only infectious things out there besides germs.

Giggles can spread from person to person.

So can blushing.
But maybe the most powerful infectious thing is the act of speaking the truth."

Vera Nazarian

Listening to truth invites truth, and clients have a way of encouraging each other to take emotional risks in the safety of the group process. As they share it is not uncommon for silliness to happen as they create interesting spins on the consequences of their addiction. They can relate in an intimate way as they share their struggle to control their alcohol and drug use, and the defenses they have created to manage the chaos in their lives. They can be real with each other call each other on what they hear, and it's powerful in a way that the same feedback in individual counseling can never be.

_____

_____

_____

_____

_____

_____

_____

_____

_____

_____

_____

"In order to grow, I promise you'll have to let go of some habits. 10 times out of 10, they'll be the habits you're most in love with."

Brandi L. Bates, Remains To Be Seen

The wisdom of the 6th and 7th step is that we acknowledge that WE can't release our character defects – we are too attached to them. It takes a Higher Power. On the other hand it may be that our character defects can also be character strengths when used in the right circumstance. It helps to talk this through with a therapist or sponsor. Some habits are more seductive than others. Maybe you struggle with control issues, pouting, busyness, or being judgmental. I certainly know how great a good bout of self-righteous anger can feel! Take a look at your emotional and behavioral habits today, and challenge yourself to make a small change. It's an experiment!

_____

_____

_____

_____

_____

_____

_____

_____

_____

_____

_____

_____

"Do it badly; do it slowly; do it fearfully; do it any way you have to, but do it."

Steve Chandler, Reinventing Yourself: How to Become the Person You've Always Wanted to Be

This is sooooo hard for a perfectionist. We want to do a lot of research, get all of our ducks in a row, and hedge our bets. It takes a lot of strength to be spontaneous, and individual and group counseling requires us to think on our feet all the time. We need to let go of the belief that there is a "right" way to do things, and to take advantaged in openings in the group process which become teachable moments. This means we have to get our self-consciousness out of the way and be completely immersed in the process ourselves. We can notice the body language and facial shifts in reaction to what is being expressed. We can invite the quiet member, the observer, to offer their insights.

_____

_____

_____

_____

_____

_____

_____

_____

_____

_____

_____

_____

_____

_____

August 28 — Gratitude

"And once the storm is over, you won't remember how you made it through, how you managed to survive. You won't even be sure, whether the storm is really over. But one thing is certain. When you come out of the storm, you won't be the same person who walked in. That's what this storm's all about."

Haruki Murakami

How different are you at this point in your life? Would people who knew you "back when" recognize you? This comes up from time to time is we work in the same community where we used and got clean. Old associates, a former sponsor, maybe someone we did time with all arrive when we least expect them. They make assumptions about who we are that can be painful reminders, and also grateful reminders of how far we have come. You may be the perfect example of what may be possible for them. If you can get your life back, maybe so can they!

_____

_____

_____

_____

_____

_____

_____

_____

_____

_____

_____

_____

"This is an important lesson to remember when you're having a bad day, a bad month, or a shitty year. Things will change: you won't feel this way forever. And anyway, sometimes the hardest lessons to learn are the ones your soul needs most. I believe you can't feel real joy unless you've felt heartache. You can't have a sense of victory unless you know what it means to fail. You can't know what it's like to feel holy until you know what it's like to feel really fucking evil. And you can't be birthed again until you've died."

Kelly Cutrone C. JoyBell C.

Change is the only certainty in life. We have to work hard to prevent change from happening – it takes something drastic like drug abuse or alcoholism to keep up frozen in time. The minute we wake up again life begins moving forward, only it includes us instead of happens around us. The pace of life can be scary at first, especially if we referred sedatives! Our past provides the perspective that allows us to hang in there for the ride. You are where you are supposed to be.

"Certain things in life simply have to be experienced -and never explained. Love is such a thing."

Paulo Coelho, Maktub

There are different kinds of learning styles. Some of us are visual, some of us are auditory, and some of us are kinesthetic. Experiential learning can permanently shift our perspective, and we retain what we learn at an almost cellular level. I can intellectually understand that you love me. However, as long as I'm convinced that I'm not loveable then I will not feel loved. We could only understand recovery when we truly entered it and maintained it for several months. We stayed sober long enough to experience what it felt like to be a recovering person and as well as the benefits of our new life. Allowing people in our life to love us until we can love ourselves is crucial to making the shift happen. At some point we will FEEL loved.

_____

_____

_____

_____

_____

_____

_____

_____

_____

_____

_____

_____

"The right thing to do is so easy to see when you're seventeen years old and don't have to make any big decisions. When you know that no matter what you do, someone will take care of you and fix everything. But when you're grown up, the world is not that black and white, and the right thing doesn't a tidy little arrow pointing to it."

Huntley Fitzpatrick, My Life Next Door

When our clients were seventeen it's possible that they were loaded, and the biggest decision they had to make was where they were going to party and who's bringing the stuff? Unfortunately, they may have freeze-framed this, and made very few decisions in adulthood that weren't a reaction to something they could no longer avoid. We will need to teach them an organized decision-making process to help them sort out decisions they have to make in sobriety. It will help to do this if we are practicing good decision making skills ourselves.

"I always laugh at the term 'Cinderella story', because, if you ask me, it doesn't matter what life you're living, life never has a solution. No matter how hard the struggles are that you leave behind, new struggles always take their place."

Chris Colfer, The Wishing Spell

Many clients have an expectation that once they are clean and sober they'll get back the life they lost. Their wife will come back, they'll get a better job, and they'll get their children back. We know from years of experience that it doesn't always work this way, and magical thinking can be a huge set-up for relapse. We need to temper the "pink cloud" and new hope with realistic markers of success that don't depend on other people's choices. It's heartbreaking when the bridge has been burned too badly, and the client will have to make peace with this fact. Some of us have done this, and can reassure them that acceptance is the only path to serenity.

"That was when I first observed a phenomenon I now call the "New York Slide": you offer your words to try to communicate and connect with someone, but your words just hit a brick wall the person has erected to ward off human contact- the words slide down it and roll away."

Kelly Cutrone, If You Have to Cry, Go Outside: And Other Things Your Mother Never Told You

Our clients come in defended and locked down. They are suspicious of people "in the system," and they don't trust easily. They may not be interested in communicating, and yet our function in their treatment episode is to facilitate connection. The key is to communicate about what they value, what they need. . . "meet them where they're at," as they say. You may have to guess based on what they're wearing, or comments they make, and offer a light comment. Then you wait and see. Most people want to be seen and heard, even though they may have given up on this happening. We can surprise them with our ability to be attuned.

_____

_____

_____

_____

_____

_____

_____

_____

_____

_____

September 3 — Blame

"An important decision I made was to resist playing the Blame Game. The day I realized that I am in charge of how I will approach problems in my life, that things will turn out better or worse because of me and nobody else, that was the day I knew I would be a happier and healthier person. And that was the day I knew I could truly build a life that matters."

Steve Goodier

Blame really does get in the way when we get ready to change our lives. Yet, blame can be so satisfying sometimes. A little self-righteous indignation over the behaviors of others can drive us and give us energy that feels stronger than the sadness we're afraid of. When we take the blame we're then faced with the decision to do something about it! When we finally make the decision to make amends we'll free ourselves from the story we tell ourselves that keeps the anger stoked. Our energy can be used differently now — used to create a more satisfying life.

"It's sometimes easie. to help others rather than helping yourself. The trick is to listen to your "self" as a friend. This may be the simplest change you ever make in life, with the biggest impact."

Lorii Myers, Make It Happen, A Healthy, Competitive Approach to Achieving Personal Success

Codependency started early in life for many of us, and we find it much easier to pay attention to other people. Over time we forget to check in with ourselves, and we rarely listen to what we need and want. In some ways, we make it irrelevant. We may have used alcohol and drugs to help us stay detached from ourselves, so feelings may begin to come back when we get sober. We see this play out with clients who focus on each other instead of themselves. It's natural to be sucked into other people's drama to avoid our own reality. It takes support and redirection to change this pattern.

_____

_____

_____

_____

_____

_____

_____

_____

_____

_____

_____

_____

"If you cannot see yourself fairly or accurately represented in the community where you live... and nothing there makes you feel awake or alive, I suggest you start doing some research on some other communities"

Kelly Cutrone, If You Have to Cry, Go Outside: And Other Things Your Mother Never Told You

How are feeling about your workplace? Do you feel you belong? Are you reminded of your dysfunctional family growing up? Perhaps this includes times in staff meeting when you assume your original family role as the scapegoat or hero. Maybe you have ethical concerns. It's important to spend your days, sometimes very long days, in a setting where you feel your contribution matters. Maybe you need to address your concerns with your supervisor, or maybe you need to update your resume. If it's not the center, maybe it's you. When was the last time you took a vacation?

_____

_____

_____

_____

_____

_____

_____

_____

_____

_____

_____

_____

September 6 — Humility

"Some things need to be left unsaid."

Simone Elkeles, Wild Cards

It is a troubling habit for counselors to point out everything they see without giving the client a chance to reflect and come to their own conclusions. It reminds me of the smarty-pants kid in class who always had their hand up. "Pick me, pick me," they urged. We don't need to prove to the client that we're smart enough or have enough clean time to be competent. Perhaps we struggled in school, and going back to college to become certified was a real challenge for us. So, we have this urge to demonstrate that we belong, that we're smarter than people think. Relax, you've earned your seat. It's fine to point out patterns than clients can't see, but the more they identify about themselves the bigger the impact it will have.

_____

_____

_____

_____

_____

_____

_____

_____

_____

_____

_____

_____

_____

_____

"The wishbone will never replace the backbone"

Will Henry

This is such a clever quote! And so true. Magical thinking is a large part of the addiction lifestyle. Rather than planning or logic we rely on our instincts when we get backed against the wall. Sometimes we have strategies such as "roostering up" when we feel threatened, or distracting others when we're confronted and twisting the situation to create confusion and chaos. We believed that we would get "love" from the judge, or that our probation offer would magically let us transfer to another community. We would make our plans based on their anticipated agreement, and then became discouraged and angry when it fell through. It takes willingness and openness to plan carefully and respond instead of react. It takes emotional maturity that will develop in ongoing sobriety. We can model this when we working through case management strategies with the client.

_____

_____

_____

_____

_____

_____

_____

_____

_____

_____

September 8 — K.I.S.S.

"Big house, big car, big breast, big life, big this and big that; what is so big about living big? Live on KISS principle not BIG principle."

Santosh Kalwar

Some of us really like to live life LARGE. We over-spend, over-eat, and maybe even over-talk. Have you heard of the term, FOBO? It means Fear of Being Left Out. Maybe we're like little kids peeking down the bannister and watching the adults playing cards, wondering about their conversation and hoping to hear all the "good stuff" they never tell us. The other slogan we here frequently is Keep It Simple Stupid, which reminds us to do first things first, and keep our recovery our priority instead of fast cars and fast women! Focusing on a Big life may have led to addiction, crime, and dealing in the first place. Maybe it's time to value what you have rather than smashing your nose against the store window. Life offers so much that money can't buy.

_____

_____

_____

_____

_____

_____

_____

_____

_____

_____

_____

"I no longer have the energy for meaningless friendships, forced interactions or unnecessary conversations. If we don't vibrate on the same frequency there's just no reason for us to waste our time. I'd rather have no one and wait for substance than to not feel someone and fake the funk."

Joquesse Eugenia

Many of us spent years in relationships where we were "faking the funk," and the vibrations we were putting out drew people to us that would fake it with us. When we want to change the quality of people in our life we have to change what we offer. When we change what we offer it may shrink the pool for us to choose from, and we will need to be patient while we are waiting. When you work all the time the only people you see are coworkers and clients, and you can begin to develop inappropriate attachments to them. You need to broaden the pool you fish in, and this means expanding your life beyond work and meeting attendance.

_____

_____

_____

_____

_____

_____

_____

_____

_____

_____

_____

"Just because the boat rocks doesn't mean it's time to jump overboard."

Suzanne Woods Fisher, The Keeper

If you have suffered a lot of trauma and loss in your life, the brain changes and sensitivity to future trauma is heightened. We become acutely sensitive, and are quick to jump to the worst conclusion so we can brace ourselves for the next incoming hit. Over-reaction is hard on your adrenal system, and even when you can restore your thinking, your adrenal cascade takes longer to slow down. This is how we get systemic illness over time such as rheumatoid arthritis, fibromyalgia, migraines, and blood pressure problems. It's vital for your health that your take up a practice such as mindfulness or yoga to allow you to become less reactive and more easily restored when you do react. There are studies showing that mediation can change your brain toward compassion and joy. You deserve it!

_____
_____
_____
_____
_____
_____
_____
_____
_____
_____

SEPTEMBER 11 — A DECISION TO LIVE

"Most people don't want to die, but they don't want to live either. I am speaking about men now as much as women. They look for a third way, but there is no third way."

Jonathan Rosen, Eve's Apple: A Novel

I would disagree with the author. Addiction is a third way, a way of sleepwalking through our lives not choosing to live and not choosing to die. It's this carelessness with our own lives that saddens me. We don't know how precious we are, how much our contribution to the world matters. One of the great joys of recovery is finding a sense of commitment to living – to show up and participate in the world. Some of us chose to channel our new found purpose into working with other alcoholics and addicts which gives meaning to our suffering. We recognize the "walking dead" when we see them in the world as we're out and about living our lives. However, making a decision to fully live is a very personal one, a decision that only the client can make.

_____

_____

_____

_____

_____

_____

_____

_____

_____

_____

"Some people are like that - always searching for something better, never satisfied. Makes you wonder if they ever get a good night's sleep. They must toss and turn, dreaming about a softer mattress or a plumper pillow."

Farahad Zama, The Many Conditions of Love

The search for something new, better, shinier outside of ourselves drives a lot of addiction. We search for the better high, chase the next risk, relationship or hope to win the lottery. Even when we accomplish the risk, get the hot girl, or find a better drug the search doesn't end. There's an internal restlessness that drives us forward – I think of it as we're missing the "moderate" gene that seems to let other people rest. We can channel that drive for something more into spiritual growth or deepening relationship intimacy. It is a fact for many of us that we don't naturally gravitate toward the middle so it's a matter of giving that part of us heathy direction.

"What it taught me was forgiveness. It taught me that when people present themselves in a certain way, there's probably some back story or issue or reason for the way that they are. It's not you. It's them. And a lot of times, it's about something that's completely out of their control"

Denzel Washington, A Hand to Guide Me

Helpers instinctively seem to know this, which is why we can be patient with people that other people can barely stand to be in the room with. It's not because we're martyrs or masochistic—it's because we KNOW we've been that person at times. Defenses are rarely pretty, and they were learned for protection reasons—so the person who is defensive was under siege at some point in their life when this behavior was necessary. They don't realize they're no longer under siege, and we have a chance to let them experience the treatment process as a safe zone. They have a chance to put down their gloves and let us into their lives. It can be like holding out an oat for a deer. You stay very still and be patient.

_____

_____

_____

_____

_____

_____

_____

_____

"You ever have the feeling you were in the wrong place? That if you could just get over the next hill, cross the next river, look down into the next valley, it'd all...fit. Be right."

"All my life, more of less"

"All your life spent getting ready for the next thing. I climbed a lot of hills now. I crossed a lot of rivers. Crossed the sea even, left everything I knew and came to Styria. But there I was, waiting for me at the docks when I got off the boat, same man, same life. Next valley ain't no different from this one. No better anyway. Reckon I've learned ... just to stick in the place I'm at. Just to be the man I am."

Joe Abercrombie, Best Served Cold

There probably isn't a better marriage, better job, better neighborhood until YOU are different. Alcoholics and addicts are fond of the geographic solution to what worries us. However, recovery teaches us that we can't escape ourselves.

_____

_____

_____

_____

_____

_____

_____

_____

_____

_____

_____

_____

"I reflected that for all the people you lost touch with or couldn't hold on to, life occasionally made up for it by giving you the right person at the right time!!"

Lisa Kleypas

Clients lose valuable relationships throughout their life in addiction. Maybe they had valuable co-workers and business partners, warm neighbors, dear family members that began to separate themselves from them as their lives began to be train wrecks. Or maybe they were a functional addict and spent their time hiding a secret which made intimacy with others impossible. So, relationships would begin to drift. Some of these relationships can be repaired in recovery and time. Some are long gone, and we need to assist clients to construct new friends. They may even need to develop a new family made of accepting people in the recovering community. We know this is possible because we did this ourselves if we're in recovery.

_____

_____

_____

_____

_____

_____

_____

_____

_____

_____

_____

"A pearl is a beautiful thing that is produced by an injured life. It is the tear [that results] from the injury of the oyster. The treasure of our being in this world is also produced by an injured life. If we had not been wounded, if we had not been injured, then we will not produce the pearl."

Stephan A. Hoeller

What a beautiful analogy this is! What pearls have been created from the rubbing of sand against the injury in your life? There are "pearls of wisdom" you share with the clients in treatment so often you may not notice when it happens. You certainly notice when a co-worker orchestrates a meaningful intervention in group, or when another coworker masterfully handles a client crisis and seems to know just what to say. When we are in our "zone" working with clients we may be doing what come naturally to us, honed by education and training. It's possible your co-workers see this as well, even if they don't say so. It's enough for you to value your "pearls of great price."

"Here's one of the things I learned that morning: if you cross a line and nothing happens, the line loses meaning. It's like that old riddle about a tree falling in a forest, and whether it makes a sound if there's no one around to hear it.

You keep drawing a line farther and farther away, crossing it every time. That's how people end up stepping off the edge of the earth."

Lauren Oliver, Before I Fall

So many times we've heard clients talk about family "threats" that never seemed to transpire. In the family's desperation to stop the cycle of addiction they've threatened to cut the addict off, get a divorce, stop paying for school, fire them from the family business…. yet they were terrified that doing this would push the addict fully out of their control. Ultimately they were afraid the addict would die, a terrifying prospect for family members. For the addict, the only consequences that matter are the ones that actually take place.

_____

_____

_____

_____

_____

_____

_____

_____

_____

_____

"Nothing - not prestige, power or pride - is worth sacrificing the things that you truly want, the things that you truly love." Don't be afraid to take time and smell the roses. Don't hesitate in seeking out those things you hold dear. Seeking them out and holding on to them. And don't ever cease standing up for what you believe in, and fighting for those things that you want. Life is too short. Do what makes you happy, regardless of how others might feel."

Brenda Jackson, Taking Care of Business

We tend to either overestimate or underestimate the importance of happiness. It's pretty important for quality of life. My happy place is very different from yours, or maybe they overlap in some ways. While families tend to see addiction as "having fun," addicts and alcoholics know that it just starts out that way. The addiction lifestyle is incredibly stressful with relief coming less and less often. Recovery offers chance to build a new life, which includes adding what makes our heart happy. Are you happy?

_____

_____

_____

_____

_____

_____

_____

_____

_____

_____

_____

"Learn to recognize good luck when it's waving at you, hoping to get your attention."

Sally Koslow

What distracts us from seeing opportunity and good luck? Most of the time it's fear. We're so focused on self-protection and getting-by that we have trouble seeing the world around us. Instead of opportunity we see threat. As our clients have less and less to hide, they can begin to stop looking over their shoulders and start looking for new options. They can begin to listen and contribute to situations that open opportunities for employment or friendship. Openness is a sign of emotional and cognitive health. How about you? How well do you see opportunities and recognize good fortune when it arrives? If not I encourage you to seek out people in your life that can help you reframe and see options in situations as they unfold in your life.

_____

_____

_____

_____

_____

_____

_____

_____

_____

_____

_____

"Letting go means to come to the realization that some people are a part of your history, but not a part of your destiny."

Steve Maraboli

This is incredibly hard to do when you want someone or something with every fiber of your being. We will twist ourselves into various contortions trying to make something work that people outside of us can easily see is a "no-hoper" and still we cling. In our own way we can even get a perverse sense of pride out of being able to hang in there when everyone else would have walked away. Codependents don't need to learn to hang on, we need to let go; pull our claws out and stay in our own hula-hoop. We sometimes need people in our lives to help pull our stiff fingers off the ledge we're clinging to. It's so freeing when we finally learn this; we learn to love from a distance which is a great definition of detachment.

_____

_____

_____

_____

_____

_____

_____

_____

_____

_____

_____

_____

"When you're drowning you don't think, I would be incredibly pleased if someone would notice I'm drowning and come and rescue me. You just scream."

John Lennon

Our clients don't yell for help in obvious ways sometimes. Maybe they insist with intense emotion that they don't need help at all. Sometimes they have tantrums, or avoid attention and we can overlook them. Occasionally they self-sabotage just when they look like they're going to move forward. It's important to consider that they might be drowning when they are acting out in annoying or disruptive ways. Perhaps this is also true for you. How do people in your life know when you need help? Do you use your words or do you act it out in ways that only people paying close attention would identify? Our clients need to learn to identity when they need assistance and then learn to use their words to ask for help. It helps if YOU have this skill.

_____

_____

_____

_____

_____

_____

_____

_____

_____

_____

_____

"If complete and utter chaos was lightning, then he'd be the sort to stand on a hilltop in a thunderstorm wearing wet copper armor and shouting 'All gods are bastards!'"

Terry Pratchett, The Color of Magic

Do you have clients like this? I call him Captain Chaos and he drags chaos around him like Pig-pen in Peanuts. He can take any straightforward situation and turn it into a disaster requiring lots of energy to address. Clients like this can make our jobs exhausting, and they can be hard to live with for the rest of the clients in the treatment center. It's important to listen for what he's communicating underneath his behavior. Maybe he's stimulation seeking because he has ADHD. Maybe he has poor emotional regulation skills and can't modulate his reactions. Maybe the only people who got attention in his family demanded attention. He could also be under the influence, so don't be afraid to test him. Sometimes the answer's simpler than you think!

_____
_____
_____
_____
_____
_____
_____
_____
_____
_____
_____
_____

September 23 — Recovering men

"I suppose it's not a social norm, and not a manly thing to do — to feel, discuss feelings. So that's what I'm giving the finger to. Social norms and stuff...what good are social norms, really? I think all they do is project a limited and harmful image of people. It thus impedes a broader social acceptance of what someone, or a group of people, might actually be like."

Jess C. Scott, New Order

I had never heard men talk about their feelings until I walked into the rooms of recovery. They talked about loss, discouragement, happiness, fear . . . it blew my mind and profoundly shifted my trust for men. Traditional male gender roles have kept men encased inside themselves, unable to communicate effectively which makes them see women as curious and hard to understand. In recovery we share so much that crosses gender and simply stems from being human. In a weird way, this means we can be even better men and women. A man working a strong program is an absolute catch!

_____

_____

_____

_____

_____

_____

_____

_____

_____

_____

"Learn to drive?"
"Never," said Quentin. "My mission in life is to be a passenger."

Diana Wynne Jones, Archer's Goon

This describes a lot of people in treatment. For whatever reason their development was interrupted in the initiative stage in childhood. They feel safer being dependent and allowing others to make the major choices in their lives. Maybe they're in treatment with you because someone else placed them there. This can be a difficult client because they passively do what's asked of them but they don't initiate or show enthusiasm for their own recovery or their own life. They're vulnerable to the manipulative clients in treatment, and can get sucked into their schemes. These clients require us to be paying attention to every sign if independence they demonstrate, no matter how small. They will most likely need to go to an SLE to help them launch from the life that support their addiction.

_____

_____

_____

_____

_____

_____

_____

_____

_____

_____

"Did you ever hear one of those corny, positive messages on someone's answering machine? 'Hi, it's a great day and I'm out enjoying it right now. I hope you are too. The thought for the day is share the love. Beep.' 'Uh, yeah, this is the VD clinic... speaking of being positive, your test is back. Stop sharing the love."

Andy Rooney

I grinned when I read this, because I completely agree with Andy! I confess I find upbeat messages annoying, especially since I have to wait for them to end before I can leave my message! This reminds me of emotional intelligence for some reason. Running around declaring yourself to be "blessed" and blessing everyone in your path can be really irritating to people who feel like crap, and just need someone to get them. Invalidating them solicits an even longer list of complaints to justify their misery. Sometimes what they need to hear is, 'Wow man, that sucks" to feel understood.

_____
_____
_____
_____
_____
_____
_____
_____
_____
_____
_____
_____

September 26 — Learned behavior

"If they projected the fact that they are dangerous any harder, there would be little puddles of "danger" on the floor around them. Look, it's "danger", don't step in it!"

Mercedes Lackey, *The Eagle & the Nightingales*

Those of us who work in programs with criminal justice clients can encounter people who have mastered prison survival behaviors. These include being hard-to-read, withholding information, demanding respect and never, never snitching. This can be intimidating to counselors who don't have criminal justice histories, and who may be hesitant to confront these clients or ask them to follow the program structure. Bullies know when this behavior is working to maintain their distance, so you'll have to work through your fear to be able to be effective on your shift. Remember that this behavior is learned behavior – necessary when incarcerated but not always who they are as people. It can soften with time.

_____

_____

_____

_____

_____

_____

_____

_____

_____

_____

_____

"I'm currently unsupervised It freaks me out too but the possibilities are endless."

Darynda Jones, Fifth Grave Past the Light

Clients can really struggle, freak out, and relapse when they get close to the end of formal supervision. If they've been in the system for a long time they've always had the invisible handcuffs on their wrist. On the one hand they crave their freedom. However, the endless possibilities without direction can be overwhelming and terrifying. As a result, they may choose to remain in the system, even though this is not a conscious choice. We need to help them identify and voice this fear if it's present, which can interrupt the self-sabotage and lead to creating a realistic discharge plan. Without acknowledging their fear they will be prone to return to old playgrounds out of instinct. We need to make it safe to talk about this fear which means being comfortable with similar fears we may have had.

"I don't know the rules of grammar. If you're trying to persuade people to do something, or buy something, it seems to me you should use their language."

David Ogilvy

This is a great point. Even when we know the textbook term for what's happening, using the jargon can be distancing in the therapeutic relationship. We don't need to impress clients with our textbook knowledge – we need to connect with them at a heart level. This doesn't mean using street jargon or slang – it means speaking clearly, kindly and directly then checking to make sure you're understood. Actually this is called Active Listening, and the same skills apply to communication in general. Clear communication can create trust with the clients and our co-workers. If you think about it, being clear Is one of your favorite co-worker traits!

_____

_____

_____

_____

_____

_____

_____

_____

_____

_____

_____

_____

_____

"Do you know what I think about crying? I think some people have to learn to do it. But once you learn, once you know how to really cry, there's nothing quite like it. I feel sorry for those who don't know the trick. It's like whistling or singing."

Anne Rice, Memnoch the Devil

Some of our clients stopped crying in childhood, knowing it wouldn't do any good or maybe wanting to avoid satisfying the people who were making them cry. Their tear ducts may feel frozen or like an arid desert. We know that tears are cleansing, and release a chemical charge that can bring down our arousal system. We literally feel better, a little tired when we have experienced this release. Treatment can be a safe place to experiment with letting their guard down, letting the tears well up in their eyes until they spill down their cheeks. We need to practice being okay with tears rather than rushing in to hand them a Kleenex to stop the crying because it makes us anxious. This takes practice.

"The universe is, instant by instant, recreated anew. There is in truth no past, only a memory of the past. Blink your eyes, and the world you see next did not exist when you closed them. Therefore, the only appropriate state of the mind is surprise. The only appropriate state of the heart is joy. The sky you see now, you have never seen before. The perfect moment is now. Be glad of it."

Terry Pratchett

What a refreshing perspective! We only have now, in this moment, which is why we say in recovery, "Be where your feet are." This is easier to say than do in actual practice. However, when we think about the possibility of being surprised by the world it opens up so many possibilities. As much as we lay awake plotting and scheming to engineer particular outcomes in our life, we truly don't have that level of control. Relaxing into curiosity and surprise sounds like a much more rewarding way to live to me.

_____

_____

_____

_____

_____

_____

_____

_____

_____

_____

_____

"Some guys step on a rake in the dark, and get mad and go punch somebody. Others step on a rake in the dark and fall down laughing at themselves. I know which kind of guy I'd rather be. So do my friends."

Spider Robinson, Callahan's Crosstime Saloon

Which kind of guy are you? I am definitely the swear then fall down laughing type. Taking ourselves too seriously can be deadly and open us up to all kinds of potential resentments. We get frustrated when others don't take us as seriously as we take ourselves, and this can trigger an ongoing distance between co-workers and friends. What if you found yourself hilarious? What if you respected yourself but also knew how ridiculous you can be at times? This kind of balance keeps us sane. This is an important message for clients to get while they are with us. We never laugh at them, but with them. We can recognize opportunities for silliness that happen simply because we jump to conclusions or are careless.

_____

_____

_____

_____

_____

_____

_____

_____

_____

_____

OCTOBER 2 — SELF-CARE

"Most people want to be delivered from temptation but would like it to keep in touch."

Robert Orben

In recovery we call this a "reservation," or the acceptable exception to sobriety. Maybe it would be the death of a parent, maybe getting fired, maybe our wedding. When we work in treatment we're close to the active disease every day. We're immersed in the disease logic, surrounded by people who are still craving and scheming. It would be easy to slip into old conversations, swapping war stories, and get euphoric recall. This is the beginning of a potential relapse, and hopefully we have someone in our life who will call attention to a return of old thinking and behaviors. It takes vigilance to work in treatment. Criminal behavior and thinking is easily co-signed by the clients we work with, and it can be an enormous trigger. Working in treatment is NOT a substitute for your personal recovery. It makes your recovery even more important.

_____

_____

_____

_____

_____

_____

_____

_____

_____

_____

October 3 — Powerlessness

I have absolutely no pleasure in the stimulants in which I sometimes so madly indulge. It has not been in the pursuit of pleasure that I have periled life and reputation and reason. It has been the desperate attempt to escape from torturing memories, from a sense of insupportable loneliness and a dread of some strange impending doom."

Edgar Allan Poe

At least 50% of people in treatment at suffering from co-occurring mental health disorders. They range from PTSD, Anxiety, and Clinical Depression. Increasingly alcohol and drug counselors are being asked to deliver dual diagnosis treatment, and this can create a great deal of stress for us. Mental health treatment is not in our scope of practice, though we're called upon to make the right referrals and offer emotional regulation skills. The level of despair in this quote from Edgar Allen Poe is familiar to those of us who work with people in chronic relapse. Compassion is always helpful.

_____

_____

_____

_____

_____

_____

_____

_____

_____

_____

October 4 — Justice

"When I despair, I remember that all through history the way of truth and love have always won. There have been tyrants and murderers, and for a time, they can seem invincible, but in the end, they always fall. Think of it--always."

Mahatma Gandhi

This is an important sentiment, it allows us to release the need for immediate justice. Justice does not always seem present. Many of us have had experiences where someone seemed to "get away" with turning our lives upside down. In fact the lack of justice can torture us as we cry, "It's not fair!" I try to remember that it can be a good thing that it's not fair. In fact, I rarely get stopped for speeding or using the cell phone. I'm not held accountable for every thoughtless word or lethal thought I've had. More often than not it balances out in the end, though we don't always have the satisfaction of witnessing the justice. It's not for us to deal it out anyway – it's bigger than us.

_____

_____

_____

_____

_____

_____

_____

_____

_____

_____

_____

"Above all, don't lie to yourself. The man who lies to himself and listens to his own lie comes to a point that he cannot distinguish the truth within him, or around him, and so loses all respect for himself and for others. And having no respect he ceases to love."

Fyodor Dostoyevsky, The Brothers Karamazov

Being honest with ourselves can be tough to do. There are things about us that when acknowledged cause us shame. We avert our eyes and do our best to compartmentalize it when it occasionally slips out and we see it. Are you familiar with this this acronym?

Don't
Even
(k)No
I Am
Lying

So many of our clients are in Precontemplation about so many issues. Breaking through their denial is too harsh.

_____

_____

_____

_____

_____

_____

_____

_____

_____

_____

_____

"So you're always honest," I said.
"Aren't you?"
"No," I told him. "I'm not."
"Well, that's good to know, I guess."
"I'm not saying I'm a liar," I told him. He raised his eyebrows. "That's not how I meant it, anyways."
"How'd you mean it, then?"
"I just...I don't always say what I feel."
"Why not?"
"Because the truth sometimes hurts," I said.
"Yeah," he said. "So do lies, though."

Sarah Dessen, Just Listen

The most common reason for emotional dishonesty is fear of hurting someone's feelings. Yet, the respectful position to take in our relationships is to be honest - honest with kindness. Emotional honesty takes courage and willingness to be vulnerable. It's a risk that deepens our relationships – it's the only approach that can.

_____
_____
_____
_____
_____
_____
_____
_____
_____
_____

OCTOBER 7 — SELF-EXPRESSION

"I have learned now that while those who speak about one's miseries usually hurt, those who keep silence hurt more."

C.S. Lewis

Sometimes the depth of our loss defies words. Maybe our feelings are best described in colors, in sounds, maybe in a sketch or lyrics. Adding art to our work with clients gives them access to a way to express their internal world in ways that can't be captured in language. This doesn't require us to become art therapists – only to make the supplies available for clients to use. In the process of making a collage or writing lyrics to a song clients can begin to express what had seemed so overwhelming. After awhile they do find words to describe their experience and we have the chance to be a respectful witness to what they have been unable to say up to this point in time. What an honor. How about you? Do you have other mediums to express yourself than words?

_____

_____

_____

_____

_____

_____

_____

_____

_____

_____

*"Usually we walk around constantly believing ourselves.
"I'm okay" we say. "I'm alright". But sometimes the truth
arrives on you and you can't get it off. That's when you
realize that sometimes it isn't even an answer--it's a question. Even now, I wonder how much of my life is convinced."*

Markus Zusak, The Book Thief

When people ask us how we are during the course of
the day we most often reply, "Fine." Maybe we think
we're fine. Rarely do we stop and actually consider the
answer to that question. "I can handle it" is the man-
tra for Codependents. We stay in denial of our limitations, believing that we can move mountains to force
the outcomes we've decided are best for everyone we
love. No expense is too great, no inconvenience too
large. Meanwhile we abandon ourselves and believe
our own press about what we're doing. It's important
that professional helpers, who are prone to codependents, pay attention to this pattern.

_____
_____
_____
_____
_____
_____
_____
_____
_____
_____
_____
_____

"Our deepest fear is not that we are inadequate. Our deepest fear is that we are powerful beyond measure. It is our light, not our darkness that most frightens us. We ask ourselves, 'Who am I to be brilliant, gorgeous, talented, fabulous?' Actually, who are you not to be? You are a child of God. Your playing small does not serve the world. There is nothing enlightened about shrinking so that other people won't feel insecure around you. We are all meant to shine, as children do. We were born to make manifest the glory of God that is within us. It's not just in some of us; it's in everyone. And as we let our own light shine, we unconsciously give other people permission to do the same. As we are liberated from our own fear, our presence automatically liberates others."

Marianne Williamson, A Return to Love: Reflections on the Principles of "A Course in Miracles"

_____

_____

_____

_____

_____

_____

_____

_____

_____

_____

_____

_____

_____

_____

When we honestly ask ourselves which person in our lives mean the most to us, we often find that it is those who, instead of giving advice, solutions, or cures, have chosen rather to share our pain and touch our wounds with a warm and tender hand. The friend who can be silent with us in a moment of despair or confusion, who can stay with us in an hour of grief and bereavement, who can tolerate not knowing, not curing, not healing and face with us the reality of our powerlessness, that is a friend who cares."

Henri J.M. Nouwen, Out of Solitude: Three Meditations on the Christian Life

What a wonderful portrait of an effective helper. To be a good counselor we need to be able to tolerate ambivalence and unanswered questions. Sometimes there is no clear "Why" something has happened as badly as we want an explanation. There is a marvelous book I use with people who are suffering, "When Bad Things Happen to Good People," by Rabbi Harold Kushner. It's a comfort to people in pain.

_____

_____

_____

_____

_____

_____

_____

_____

_____

_____

_____

OCTOBER 11 — ISOLATION

"You can't stay in your corner of the Forest waiting for others to come to you. You have to go to them sometimes."

A.A. Milne, Winnie-the-Pooh

Heart-break and trauma can lead us to retreat into our own worlds for survival. We trust ourselves, and are content in our own company. Left to our own devices we would only engage with others when absolutely necessary. THEN we're dropped into a treatment center and socialization is unavoidable. The disease of addiction isolated us in profound ways and our social skills became rusty if we had developed them to start with. However, forced to engage, we see clients blossom. They begin to smile, to laugh, to participate in the group. Even when introverted by nature, they can be cajoled by more extraverted companions to join in the process. Group is a powerful balm to the loneliness of addiction. It's a joy to be part of their awakening.

_____

_____

_____

_____

_____

_____

_____

_____

_____

_____

_____

OCTOBER 12 — COMPASSION

"You can talk with someone for years, everyday, and still, it won't mean as much as what you can have when you sit in front of someone, not saying a word, yet you feel that person with your heart, you feel like you have known the person for forever.... connections are made with the heart, not the tongue."

C. JoyBell C.

While schooling is invaluable to create clinical skills and tools, education can't create a compassionate heart. Non-judgmental acceptance of others is something that helpers bring with them. It can be strengthened and developed with practice and experience, but it is part of the helper. If you're afraid clients are going to "get over" on you, and are always watching to make sure you aren't fooled your heart may become cynical. You begin to say things like, "If their mouth is moving they're lying." To be effective and create change our heart has to remain open.

_____

_____

_____

_____

_____

_____

_____

_____

_____

_____

_____

_____

"Sometimes our light goes out, but is blown again into instant flame by an encounter with another human being."

Albert Schweitzer

Our well could get really dry over time. There's no balance in our giving because it's our job to give and the client's job to take. That's the way it's supposed to go – but it can take its toll on us. Just when we feel like we're completely stripped we'll meet with our sponsor, or run into a favorite friend and we can feel our well begin to fill. Every laugh we exchange, every moment we spend sharing OUR life, every hug adds another foot of water and we're able to start the next day feeling ready to listen. It's important to help clients that are self-contained or have experienced abuse to begin to see people as part of the solution when they are struggling. Their instinct is that letting people in will make things worse. We know from our own experience that this doesn't have to be true!

OCTOBER 14 — ACCEPTANCE

"We're all seeking that special person who is right for us. But if you've been through enough relationships, you begin to suspect there's no right person, just different flavors of wrong. Why is this? Because you yourself are wrong in some way, and you seek out partners who are wrong in some complementary way. But it takes a lot of living to grow fully into your own wrongness. And it isn't until you finally run up against your deepest demons, your unsolvable problems—the ones that make you truly who you are—that we're ready to find a lifelong mate. Only then do you finally know what you're looking for. You're looking for the wrong person. But not just any wrong person: the right wrong person—someone you lovingly gaze upon and think, "This is the problem I want to have."

I will find that special person who is wrong for me in just the right way.

Let our scars fall in love."

Andrew Boyd

_____

_____

_____

_____

_____

_____

_____

_____

_____

_____

_____

_____

OCTOBER 15 — CLINICAL ALLIANCE

"Stories never really end...even if the books like to pretend they do. Stories always go on. They don't end on the last page, any more than they begin on the first page."

Cornelia Funke, Inkspell

One of the more challenging aspects of working in treatment is that we enter people's lives in the middle of their life stories, and they leave us way before the story ends. For the most part we never know how things turn out. Do they stay married? Are they still sober? Did they have children? We have to get good at jumping in the middle of the story without knowing the beginning and picking our way through to figure out the backstory. We work our way through this with the client, so it's a joint discovery. We can work with the present chapter in a client's life – this is where we have our influence and reframe their story to include elements that are more likely to lead to a happy ending. But when the client leaves us we never really know, do we?

"The unreal is more powerful than the real. Because nothing is as perfect as you can imagine it. Because its only intangible ideas, concepts, beliefs, fantasies that last. Stone crumbles. Wood rots. People, well, they die. But things as fragile as a thought, a dream, a legend, they can go on and on. If you can change the way people think. The way they see themselves. The way they see the world. You can change the way people live their lives. That's the only lasting thing you can create."

Chuck Palahniuk, Choke

This is what we do day in and day out. When we help people change the way they think the whole course of their lives, as well as the lives of the people they love, can be altered. This is a heavy responsibility when you think about it, and also a great privilege. What we say and how we say it creates a safe place for people to heal, regroup, and consider hard choices they need to make going forward. What we do matters.

_____

_____

_____

_____

_____

_____

_____

_____

_____

_____

_____

_____

"There must be those among whom we can sit down and weep and still be counted as warriors."

Adrienne Rich

We need people in our lives who can hear our discouragement with clients, or see our overwhelm at the mounting paperwork, and not worry that we're not competent. In fact, competence requires us to be aware of our counter-transference and limitations and talk about them honestly on the way to finding strategies and solutions. Hopefully your co-workers or Clinical Supervisor are able to provide this safe place to process your feelings about your reactions to the clients. Mostly, it's important that you not judge yourself harshly when you are tired or feel frustrated at work. We are providing treatment to people who may not see the value in what we do, so it's important that WE see the value in what we do. This kind of support is not optional if we want to avoid burnout. Do you have this support team?

_____

_____

_____

_____

_____

_____

_____

_____

_____

_____

_____

"I've known people that the world has thrown everything at to discourage them...to break their spirit. And yet something about them retains a dignity. They face life and don't ask quarters."

Horton Foote

The resilience of the clients we meet never ceases to amaze me. More than that, it touches and nudges me to keep my perspective when my own life is challenging. One of the strongest and most effective approaches to working with addicts is a strengths-based approach. We look for the exceptions to the problem, times when they've dealt well with adversity. We look toward skills and strengths they already have rather than thinking they need to change everything about them to be successful. There are survival skills that will be invaluable in helping the stay sober over the long haul. Our job is to point these out, or reframe character deficits into character strengths used correctly. It's as though we become strengths detectives!

_____

_____

_____

_____

_____

_____

_____

_____

_____

_____

October 19 — Spiritual actions

"I sought to hear the voice of God and climbed the topmost steeple, but God declared: "Go down again - I dwell among the people."

John Henry Newman

We are encouraged in the Twelfth step to "practice these principles in all our affairs," not just in the rooms. Service, a major feature of long term successful recovery, allows us to be the arms and legs of the Higher Power. We can go to court with the client for support, or sit at night with the client who can't sleep during detox. In those moments, we can extend the compassion and acceptance that may be closest to spiritual experience they have ever had. Many people struggle with the God part of the program because it seems unreal and magical. Service to other clients, like teaching them to do a chore or helping them with their assignments aligns them with spirituality in their actions if not their belief system. Spirituality can be an experience, belief or an action. We can choose spiritual behaviors.

_____

_____

_____

_____

_____

_____

_____

_____

_____

"When things break, it's not the actual breaking that prevents them from getting back together again. It's because a little piece gets lost - the two remaining ends couldn't fit together even if they wanted to. The whole shape has changed."

John Green, Will Grayson, Will Grayson

We are never the same when leave our addiction behind. At first families just want clients "to get sober, and assume everything will be the same only better because the alcohol is gone. But recovery is a much broader process, and requires clients' to examine themselves closely. They begin to change the way they think and the way they interact with others Maybe they set boundaries for the first time in their lives, or refuse to participate in someone else's drama. This can be strange for people who know them, and family may even push back or call the client selfish for taking care of themselves. Maybe you experienced this in your own recovery, which makes you a great source of reality testing.

_____

_____

_____

_____

_____

_____

_____

_____

_____

_____

"If we listened to our intellect we'd never have a love affair. We'd never have a friendship. We'd never go in business because we'd be cynical: "It's gonna go wrong." Or "She's going to hurt me." Or, "I've had a couple of bad love affairs, so therefore . . ." Well, that's nonsense. You're going to miss life. You've got to jump off the cliff all the time and build your wings on the way down."

Ray Bradbury

The best decisions are made from the combination of both head and heart. Some of us don't trust our heart- we are suspect of emotions so rarely even consult with our heart or gut instinct. Do you know you have a vegus nerve that connects your amygdala to your gut? This is the biological explanation for "gut instinct." We sense and feel first then our head labels and identifies what we're feeling. This is way we can get a feeling way before we get information that supports the feeling we had. We need to consult with both head and heart to really KNOW.

_____
_____
_____
_____
_____
_____
_____
_____
_____
_____

"How would your life be different if... You stopped making negative judgmental assumptions about people you encounter? Let today be the day... You look for the good in everyone you meet and respect their journey."

Steve Maraboli, Life, the Truth, and Being Free

This is your challenge for today. This includes your annoying and bossy co-workers, conflict-seeking clients', and cranky family members. Sometimes it can be hard to see the good in people when their behavior is intrusive. This is why knowing the backstory can help us take a deep breath, pray for patience, and continue wading into the encounter. It helps to deliberately look for points of agreement or quirks that are interesting if not endearing. Everyone was someone's child at some point, and this is especially true for our clients because they are often still child-like in their approach to situations. They are often coming from a magical thinking perspective, and if you see the child in their eyes it might help you to hold your tongue.

_____

_____

_____

_____

_____

_____

_____

_____

_____

_____

_____

"By choosing recovery and risking to be real, we set the healthy boundaries that say, "I am in charge of my recovery and my life, and no one else on this Earth is."

Charles L. Whitfield

There are times when clients really want to be in charge, especially when they want to manipulate the outcome of situations. Ironically, they don't seem to want to be responsible for themselves. Being in charge of themselves and their recovery raises the stakes, and they get afraid they'll blow it. A treatment center staff has the chance to create an alliance with a client that will help them have the courage to go ahead and own their own life. While they're powerless over their addiction, they can use their new energy and focus to manage everything else. Maintaining our own mental and emotional health requires us to make our recovery and personal life a priority. Healthy boundaries are key to our sanity.

OCTOBER 24 — SELF-ACCEPTANCE

*"Each person you meet
is an aspect of yourself,
clamoring for love."*

Eric Micha'el Leventhal

There are so many parts of us that we have deemed unacceptable Maybe we judge ourselves and other people harshly who seem "needy." Maybe we complain about our "lazy" coworker, or self-centered relative. Carl Jung explored what he called the shadow" in great depth. The shadow is made up of the qualities about ourselves that we deny are part of us. So, we judge other people who display these qualities, and may even project these qualities on other people. If I think it's not okay to be angry, I'm going to read other people as angry even when they aren't. Jung tells us that we need to accept those dark parts and learn to appreciate all of who we are, not just the "good parts." How are you doing with ALL of you?

"I feel like, God expects me to be human. I feel like, God likes me just the way I am: broken and empty and bruised. I feel like, God doesn't look at me and wish that I were something else, because He likes me just this way. I feel like, God doesn't want me to close my eyes and pray for Him to make me holy or for Him to make me pure; because He made me human. I feel like, God already knows I'm human...it is I who needs to learn that."

C. JoyBell

What an intimate description of her relationship with her Higher Power. She has an acceptance and compassion for her humanity that comes from a secure attachment with her Higher Power. What if this description were accurate - that God doesn't want us to be other than we are. It would make sense - in our imperfection we need a Higher Power because we recognize that we aren't in control, and managing ourselves when the anxiety increases requires assistance. It's worth considering.

_____

_____

_____

_____

_____

_____

_____

_____

_____

"At the end of the day, it's not about what you have or even what you've accomplished. It's about what you've done with those accomplishments. It's about who you've lifted up, who you've made better. It about what you've given back."

Denzel Washington, A Hand to Guide Me

It's true that sharing our recovery can make it feel richer and more fulfilling. We all have different types of gifts that we bring to the treatment center. These gifts can range from being kind, good with our hands, motivating, good with paperwork, being resourceful, patience, teaching and laughter. Many of us are not used to thinking about ourselves in terms of gifts, and may take what we offer for granted because it comes so easily to us. If you think about the way others talk about you, or the role you play in stituations you'll have a hint. Our gifts were given to us to be used. In recovery we have the chance to share them with people who really need what we have.

OCTOBER 27 — SURRENDER

"When your footsteps and thoughts carry you down the same path your heart and soul are directing you, you will know without a doubt that you are headed in the right direction."

Molly Friedenfeld

One of dilemmas of a spiritual seeker is knowing when we're aligned with our Higher Power's will or are running on our own. It's easy to get confused about this, especially when what we want seems like it will benefit lots of other people. However road blocks are huge indicator that you may be pushing a rock up a hill. It's true that the path is not always smooth, but there is a certain flow that happens when things are unfolding as they should. Our clients have a lot of experience forcing and pushing their will and continue this pattern in treatment. We can help them learn that surrender reaches beyond their drug of choice – and teach them to learn to drop the rope and use their energy on their own behalf.

_____

_____

_____

_____

_____

_____

_____

_____

_____

_____

"You need to trust
To surrender
To ask for guidance
Go within for the answers
They're within you
You have the answers
All you need do is ask"

Karen Hackel, The Whisper of Your Soul

Is this true for you? We have to inhabit our bodies to be able to feel our response to situations. Many of us hide in our heads and rely on our thinking, so if a situation doesn't seem logical we dismiss it. We may not respect the power of the head-heart connection. We have so much wisdom that's been there all along. We have instincts that tell us who's safe and unsafe, and we choose to ignore them. We all have this inner wisdom, and we can practice listening to it. This is the gift of the 11th Step which encourages us to be still and hear ourselves. Some treatment centers include meditation or mindfulness as part of their program. What do you think?

_____

_____

_____

_____

_____

_____

_____

_____

_____

"The greatest thing you will ever give to the world is your commitment to leave what you find in better condition than the way you found it. Leave a single light in a place where there was once darkness so those coming behind you may see further and begin where you left."

Tonny K. Brown

There are those of us who used be a tornado in the lives of people. We left behind a trail of wreckage for people caught up in our chaos. If some of those people were to meet us in our recovery, they would be shocked. I have had students tell me over the years that they want to right a karmic balance by becoming a counselor and changing the impact they make on the world. This is a powerful reason to enter the addiction field or any field of service. Life offers us a chance to symbolically "undo" bad decisions sometimes, and it's exciting that we've been given the opportunity. It's possible that without your wreckage you would not be offering the quality of intervention you can offer now.

_____

_____

_____

_____

_____

_____

_____

_____

_____

OCTOBER 30 — PINK CLOUD

"Thought I wanted overnight success, until I achieved it through hard work and the refusal to back down! What you earn, you keep."

A.M. Hudson

So many people enter treatment hoping to be "struck wonderful" and magically be relieved of their cravings and additive nature. While Bill W. experienced a bright light, he had to work to keep his sobriety. It's true that sometimes our clients experience a "pink cloud" and it does feel magical. They lose their desire to use drugs and alcohol and feel better physically than they have in years. It can feel like magic. We know that this won't last, but I usually encourage them to enjoy this period, reminding them that they need to continue to learn the skills and strategies they need to keep their new sobriety. How about you? Are you continuing to work on your recovery – maybe you've been working on a something you do in your relationships that keeps getting you in trouble? Effort pays off

OCTOBER 31 — SELF-CARE

"Emerge; don't cower.
Endure; don't run.
Nurture; don't abandon"

Raji Lukkoor

Let's unpack this beautiful saying. We're encouraged to stay present and not hide in our lives. We need to stay awake! If we endure it means we stay in the game, we keep participating even when it's hard and challenging because we KNOW we don't have to do life alone. Finally we're encouraged to nurture ourselves; meet our emotional, physical intellectual, and spiritual needs. Great advice, right? Are you doing these on a regular basis? Life can get in the way of self-care – or we let other people's needs and wants take precedence. Maybe that client needs to wait until you take your lunch to meet with you. Maybe you need to return that P.O. phone call tomorrow because it's time to go home. It's important to treat yourself as though you matter.

_____

_____

_____

_____

_____

_____

_____

_____

_____

_____

_____

We're so engaged in doing things
to achieve purposes of outer value
that we forget the inner value,
the rapture that is associated
with being alive, is what it is all about.

Joseph Campbell

This can be a challenge for those of us like myself who tend to lose ourselves in our work. We can have such a passion for what we do that we forget that there's value in our inner world, our inner experiences. Our clients are very externally focused, with very real consequences and worries that preoccupy them and distract them from treatment. Part of our clinical skill is to draw attention to their inner world and validate its importance. What they feels does matter, what they need matters. It may be the first time they ever consider their internal world at all! It helps if we value our own infernal experience.

_____

_____

_____

_____

_____

_____

_____

_____

_____

_____

_____

_____

NOVEMBER 2 — FLEXIBILITY

The very nature of the world is constant change.
You set a goal and create a plan to achieve it;
then the assumptions on which you
based your plan change - they always do.
The challenge is to retain your goals
while adapting your tactics.
Relax and stay flexible in order to reach
your goals and maintain your happiness.

Jonathan Lockwood Huie

We are exposed to many different theories of counseling in school to prepare us to be flexible in our approach to people base on their world view and learning style. This flexibility is necessary rigidity in our approach with clients can hinder our success dramatically. For example, using the same counseling style with every single client, especially if it includes oversharing about your own recovery, hinders the client's recovery and leaves you ineffective. It's important to trust your training so you don't have to step into your sponsor shoes to do your job. Flexibility in life is an invaluable skill.

_____

_____

_____

_____

_____

_____

_____

_____

"The opposite of love is not hate, it's indifference. The opposite of art is not ugliness, it's indifference. The opposite of faith is not heresy, it's indifference. And the opposite of life is not death, it's indifference."

Elie Wiesel

Some of us have protected ourselves from heartache for many years by adopting an indifferent response to people and situations. We never fully ante up, and take an observational position. We are never fully present or invested to avoid disappointment or emotional risks. And it works. On the other hand we use 4 crayons in a 64 crayon box, and wind up always being on the outside of life. It takes courage to use the other colors and have stake in the game. When you are invested your have more energy, more vitality, and attract better companions. How many crayons are you using in your box?

_____

_____

_____

_____

_____

_____

_____

_____

_____

_____

_____

_____

NOVEMBER 4 — LISTENING

"You talk when you cease to be at peace with your thoughts."

Khalil Gibran, The Prophet

Counselors often struggle with silence. We get anxious and feel like we need to say or do something, and begin to fill in the gap by asking questions or telling a story. This quote is a good pointer because it reminds it that it's hard to think when're talking! This is true for clients as well, and so they need small bits of silence to process their thoughts and feelings. They have to sift through what is being said by themselves or maybe someone else in group, and it's wise to let them have their own thoughts. Providing space for people to think is just as valuable as anything we might say. We need quiet time to process as well. This is an argument for taking your lunch and breaks so you can get free from the talking for a short time and gather your own thoughts.

_____

_____

_____

_____

_____

_____

_____

_____

_____

_____

_____

November 5 — Acceptance

"The reasonable man adapts himself to the world: the unreasonable one persists in trying to adapt the world to himself. Therefore all progress depends on the unreasonable man."

George Bernard Shaw, Man and Superman

It can be hard to tell when we need to stand our ground even if makes someone else uncomfortable, and when we need to move into acceptance of a situation. Some of us are more flexible than others by nature, so our easygoing persona may make holding a boundary hard for us. Boundaries are crucial for clients because they have very few internal or external boundaries of their own. We have to teach them how to be appropriate which means they need feedback. On the other hand, some of us are more stubborn than others, and can approach situations like a puppy with a sock. Are you locked in place by a principle or by pride and ego?

_____

_____

_____

_____

_____

_____

_____

_____

_____

_____

_____

"I must say a word about fear. It is life's only true opponent. Only fear can defeat life. It is a clever, treacherous adversary, how well I know. It has no decency, respects no law or convention, shows no mercy. It goes for your weakest spot, which it finds with unnerving ease. It begins in your mind, always ... so you must fight hard to express it. You must fight hard to shine the light of words upon it. Because if you don't, if your fear becomes a wordless darkness that you avoid, perhaps even manage to forget, you open yourself to further attacks of fear because you never truly fought the opponent who defeated you."

Yann Martel, Life of Pi

Left to our own thoughts some of us can go to very dark places. We future-trip and our bodies begin to reflect our thoughts. We become fatigues, preoccupied, even clumsy when we are afraid. When we air our thoughts with someone we trust we can regain our balance and see situations more realistically.

_____

_____

_____

_____

_____

_____

_____

_____

_____

_____

_____

November 7 — Hope

"Sometimes I lie awake at night and I ask, "Is life a multiple choice test or is it a true or false test?" ...Then a voice comes to me out of the dark and says, "We hate to tell you this but life is a thousand word essay."

Charles M. Schulz

This struck me as hilarious! We are so often asking the wrong question – and then frustrated when the answers don't seem to help. Sometimes the situation is more involved and complicated than we imagine when we first enter it, and addressing it will be more like untangling a necklace than putting things in order. When we listen to clients' express their worries and fears it might be helpful if we question their assumptions from time to time, because that could shift the entire focus on the conversation in a more optimistic directions. Even when it doesn't we're least talking about the ACTUAL problem which has more hope of resolution.

_____

_____

_____

_____

_____

_____

_____

_____

_____

_____

_____

"Is it possible, in the final analysis, for one human being to achieve perfect understanding of another? We can invest enormous time and energy in serious efforts to know another person, but in the end, how close can we come to that person's essence? We convince ourselves that we know the other person well, but do we really know anything important about anyone?"

Haruki Murakami, The Wind-Up Bird Chronicle

This is a humbling reminder that we can never fully see into another person's heart. That's why saying, "I know what you feel" is such a silly and unhelpful thing to say. We all have hidden parts of ourselves, sometimes hidden to us and sometimes hidden from other people. In some ways it doesn't matter how well we understand the clients as much as assisting them to understand themselves. In the process of helping them see into their internal world we get glimpses that make them more clearly to us, and sometimes we eve recognize ourselves!

_____

_____

_____

_____

_____

_____

_____

_____

_____

_____

_____

"It's not all bad. Heightened self-consciousness, apartness, an inability to join in, physical shame and self-loathing—they are not all bad. Those devils have been my angels. Without them I would never have disappeared into language, literature, the mind, laughter and all the mad intensities that made and unmade me."

Stephen Fry, Moab Is My Washpot

Clients will occasionally express gratitude for the dark periods in their life. Maybe they experimented with music or art, join bands or took odd jobs because they were loaded. And they learned some things about themselves. Our lives have not been wasted because we were loaded; there were strengths and resilience being developed in order to survive the chaos and struggle of the addiction lifestyle. We can help clients salvage the valuable remnants of their life experience which can restore some of the dignity lost in the course of their struggle.

November 10 — Patience

"I shiver, thinking how easy it is to be totally wrong about people-to see one tiny part of them and confuse it for the whole, to see the cause and think it's the effect or vice versa"

Lauren Oliver, Before I Fall

This is so true, isn't it? And we've all done it. We draw conclusions about people when we first meet people and once we've drawn these conclusions it take a lot of evidence to change our minds! This can be frustrating to the recovering addict and alcoholic, because they so badly want to have their hard won changes recognized and acknowledged. Yet family and friends may not see them, or discount the changes because they are wedded to their previous view of the person. We can help clients be patient with this and even help them see how they do it with the other clients. How many times have they met another clients and drawn a conclusion that later tuned out to be false? We need patience with ourselves.

_____

_____

_____

_____

_____

_____

_____

_____

_____

_____

_____

"The seed of suffering in you may be strong, but don't wait until you have no more suffering before allowing yourself to be happy."

Thích Nhất Hạnh

Maybe we believe that we have to be completely at peace in order to be happy. We look for the complete absence of frustration or disappointment, and withhold opportunities for joy due to that imperfection. How can I be happy if he is still drinking? How can I be happy if my kid is struggling in school? If we're Codependent we may believe that happiness in the face of someone else's unhappiness may not be loving, and that we need to be miserable with them in solidarity. Alanon frees us from this belief – that we can be happy, joyous and free despite someone's drinking. We can live our lives with loving detachment, knowing that allowing someone to have the dignity of their choices is the most respectful position we can make.

_____

_____

_____

_____

_____

_____

_____

_____

_____

_____

_____

"For me, I am driven by two main philosophies: know more today about the world than I knew yesterday and lessen the suffering of others. You'd be surprised how far that gets you."

Neil deGrasse Tyson

What a great mission statement for life. There was book written years ago, *Seven Habits of Highly Effective People* by Stephen Covey. He recommends that we create a life mission statement, and then align our goals and activities against this mission statement. Is what I am doing with my time matching my mission? Do my goals move me closer to mission? This is a helpful suggestion because it helps us not lose our way when we are offered all kinds of possible distractions. We then have a reference point by which to make decisions. How about you? If you were going to create a short mission statement for your life, what would it be? Are your activities matching your mission?

_____

_____

_____

_____

_____

_____

_____

_____

_____

_____

_____

NOVEMBER 13 — HUMILITY

"If anyone tells you that a certain person speaks ill of you, do not make excuses about what is said of you but answer, "He was ignorant of my other faults, else he would not have mentioned these alone."

Epictetus

This quote made me smile. Wouldn't this be a great response to news that someone's hating on you? What if we offered additional flaws for them to discuss? This response requires humility and a sense of humor about yourself. The program tells us that what people think about us is none of our business, but as human beings connected to other human beings this is harder than it sounds. Our clients gossip about each other all the time. People bond with gossip – they can have a shared enemy which is often a staff member! We have to learn to shake this off, knowing it's part of their process to avoid looking at themselves. Look for the grain of truth, and let the rest go.

_____

_____

_____

_____

_____

_____

_____

_____

_____

_____

_____

_____

"People know what they do; frequently they know why they do what they do; but what they don't know is what what they do does."

Michel Foucault, Madness and Civilization: A History of Insanity in the Age of Reason

We don't always see the impact of the decisions we make. We do the best we can and unbeknownst us we may have made an observation that the clients will carry with them for years. Maybe we were part of the client's recovery and later their children don't act on their own addiction. We do a lot good, plant a lot of seeds, that we don't see grow to fruition. We have to trust that the ripple effect from the kindness we give and compassion we extend will have an impact of the clients and their families going forward. Kindness and compassion affects us in important ways. Being a kind person, sharing compassion actually extends our lives and slows our aging. So we also have long time impact from our work!

*"When you realize there is something you don't under-
stand, then you're generally on the right path to understanding all kinds of things."*

Jostein Gaarder, The Solitaire Mystery

Being teachable is a strong indicator of intelligence,
I think, because it requires curiosity which is a hallmark of intelligence. Being teachable means that
you're open to new ideas, being challenged on your
current ideas, and you welcome diversity and alternative approaches. When you have confidence you are
cognitively flexible – not threatened by new ideas or
perspectives. You can take what you like and leave
the rest. There is no one technique or approach that
works for all clients, so the goal is to grow your tool
bag to accommodate more and more clients. It's good
a thing that we're required to receive continuing education as counselors because we aren't able to avoid
learning new things which might be our instinct.

_____

_____

_____

_____

_____

_____

_____

_____

_____

_____

_____

_____

"I am a sick man... I am a spiteful man. I am an unpleasant man. I think my liver is diseased. However, I don't know beans about my disease, and I am not sure what is bothering me. I don't treat it and never have, though I respect medicine and doctors. Besides, I am extremely superstitious, let's say sufficiently so to respect medicine. . . No, I refuse to treat it out of spite. You probably will not understand that. Well, but I understand it. Of course I can't explain to you just whom I am annoying in this case by my spite. I am perfectly well aware that I cannot "get even" with the doctors by not consulting them. I know better than anyone that I thereby injure only myself and no one else. But still, if I don't treat it, it is out of spite. My liver is bad, well then-- let it get even worse!"

Fyodor Dostoyevsky, Notes from Underground

Anyone who's ever worked in treatment has seen this perverse spite – and our experience of it ourselves gives us patience with this irrational thinking. Are you still spiteful in your recovery?

_____
_____
_____
_____
_____
_____
_____
_____
_____
_____
_____
_____

"However I look and sound, whatever I say and do, and whatever I think and feel at a given moment in time is authentically me. If later some parts of how I looked, sounded, thought, and felt turn out to be unfitting, I can discard that which is unfitting, keep the rest, and invent something new for that which I discarded. I can see, hear, feel, think, say, and do. I have the tools to survive, to be close to others, to be productive, and to make sense and order out of the world of people and things outside of me. I own me, and therefore, I can engineer me. I am me, and I am Okay."

Virginia Satir

Virginia Satir reminds us that we are equipped with the ability to access our senses and thoughts to not just survive in the world but to continue to grow and change. When it comes down to it we are the only human being we can control, and sometimes that can be dicey. Becoming our best friend is crucial for serenity.

_____

_____

_____

_____

_____

_____

_____

_____

_____

_____

_____

_____

NOVEMBER 18 — SURRENDER

"The more you struggle to live, the less you live. Give up the notion that you must be sure of what you are doing. Instead, surrender to what is real within you, for that alone is sure....you are above everything distressing."

Baruch Spinoza

It's important to be reminded that we exist apart from our problems. When you've been struggling for a long time, maybe with depression or addiction, it's easy to over-identify with the struggle. We say, "Hi, my name is Mary and I'm depressed," as though that's the sum total of who we are. We are not our disease, our job, roles, and our friends. Asking ourselves who we are apart from these things can cause anxiety because while they may be ways that we express who we are in the world, they are not US. This means that when you're in the middle of a pile of crap, YOU are not crap. It's a comforting thought.

"You know how the tightrope guy at the circus wants every-one to believe his act is an art, but deep down you can see that he's really just hoping he makes it all the way across?"

Jodi Picoult, My Sister's Keeper

Sometimes we feel like we're teetering on the edge of our sanity when on the outside we look like we're making our lives work. It can be painful to have this secret, and dread someone's going to look behind the curtain and see who we really are. The hardest secret for a counselor to keep is relapse, and working in treatment while using at home can be its own kind of hell. That's why these counselors either leave or wind up using with the clients to share the pain. When a co-worker returns to the disease their behavior and atti-tude began to change before they ever picked up, so when we look back at it we can see the signs. We don't want to see the signs as they're happening. When this happens it's a time for compassion and not judgment.

_____

_____

_____

_____

_____

_____

_____

_____

_____

_____

_____

_____

"A hero is not known by the number of battles he has won, but rather by the kind of battles he chooses to fight."

Tonny K. Brown

What matters enough to you that you would fight for it? Some of us have a low threshold for the fight, and see a lot of situations as a cause for battle. Others of us have a high threshold, and it takes a lot to make us step up to the fight. You certainly see this in the clients, and a considerable amount of time is spent in treatment addressing the chaos caused by the low threshold people! Reactivity can be a strategy we use to keep people at a distance, and recovery allows us to begin to dismantle our walls and become more responsive than reactive. This doesn't mean there are never battles, because there are times when righteous anger is called for. The difference is that we can be responsive and purposeful in the way we attack a problem. Our chance of success goes way up!

_____

_____

_____

_____

_____

_____

_____

_____

_____

_____

NOVEMBER 21 — CAPACITY FOR CHANGE

"I've never met a person, I don't care what his condition, in whom I could not see possibilities. I don't care how much a man may consider himself a failure. I believe in him, for he can change the thing that is wrong in his life any time he is ready and prepared to do it. Whenever he develops the desire he can take away from his life the thing that is defeating it. The capacity for reformation and change lies within."

Preston Bradley

This is a hopeful position to take, and a position recognized by many of us who work in the addiction field. Our own healing leads us to believe that healing is possible. We also know that some of our clients face larger challenges than simply the desire to change. Co-occurring mental illness is often present, at least 50% of the time. If we primarily work with criminal justice clients the numbers are even higher. So, along with desire they're going to need resources and support. We can do this gladly.

NOVEMBER 22 — LISTENING

"Anyway, the trick is simply this: No matter what happens, keep your heart open. Wide open. The heart is made of love, and love is indestructible, and only the arrogance of ego would presume that it requires protection. To open your heart is to reduce your ego, and this is the only magic that is ever required to experience the naked truth."

Tony Vigorito, Nine Kinds of Naked

This has not always been our experience if we were lost in addiction. We encountered people and situations that may have taught us to develop survival skills to stay safe. Dismantling these skills can take time and we never fully lose them. We simply replace them with more updated beliefs in our ability to manage our heart knowing that we no longer need a wall to be safe. We need to remain open-hearted with our clients as well, which doesn't mean that we drop our boundaries. It means that if we listen closely to what they don't say, we will hear THEIR heart.

"I don't so much mind looking back on having lost the election, or having been denied a role in the play, or having had my novel repeatedly rejected, or having been turned down for a date, or recalling laughter at my expense when I attempted some silly challenge. Those things simply prove that I lived life. What I do mind, however, is looking back on the lost opportunities where imagined concerns kept me from even trying—lose or win. I've learned that there is no regret in a brave attempt, only in cowering to fear."

Richelle E. Goodrich

Our imagination can be a powerful ally or terrible opponent. Our body is intricately connected to our mind, so when we imagine being on a beach we can relax. When we imagine trying and failing our adrenal system can jack up, our heart races, and we can feel sick. We can choose our focus. We can picture success, we can picture positive outcomes, and we can picture surviving the risk because we've developed a support system.

"Life is not about how fast you start, but how the end is going to be, so don't worry when others are ahead of you just keep on doing what you have been doing."

lexis smigz

Our clients can become preoccupied with how far behind their peers they are. Once they're awake they realize that other people in their age groups have started families, have careers, and have been building their futures while they were holed up in a crack house. This can be incredibly painful, and we see them create over-compensating plans like working three jobs, or taking 21 units in school to make up for lost time. Long term recovery take patience, patience with what seems like a slow process. Maybe it means changing careers and going back to school. Maybe it means a physical rehabilitation plan due to traumatic brain injury. The important piece is to keep moving forward at a realistic and reasonable pace that we can sustain. Oh, and humility will help.

_____

_____

_____

_____

_____

_____

_____

_____

_____

_____

"I've learned that the universe doesn't care what our motives are, only our actions. So we should do things that will bring about good, even if there is an element of selfishness involved. Like the kids at my school might join the Key Club or Future Business Leaders of America, because it's a social thing and looks good on their record, not because they really want to volunteer at the nursing home. But the people at the nursing home still benefit from it, so it's better that the kids do it than not do it. And if they never did it, then they wouldn't find out that they actually liked it."

Wendy Mass, 13 Gifts

In recovery we frequently encourage newcomers to "act as if" they are in recovery, and do the next right thing regardless of how they feel about it. This is importance discipline to develop. Someone doesn't have to want to set up chairs to be willing to do it anyway. And afterwards, they see the results of their service. Our motives can be complicated, but still helpful.

_____

_____

_____

_____

_____

_____

_____

_____

_____

_____

_____

"The way I see it, our natural human instinct is to fight or flee that which we perceive to be dangerous. Although this mechanism evolved to protect us, it serves as the single greatest limiting process to our growth. To put this process in perspective and not let it rule my life,
I expect the unexpected;
make the unfamiliar familiar;
make the unknown known;
make the uncomfortable comfortable;
believe the unbelievable."

Charles F. Glassman, Brain Drain The Breakthrough That
Will Change Your Life

Recovery is a huge life adjustment, and so much of the way we see the world and operate in it has to change. Our fear mechanisms have been in overdrive, and most of us enter the recovery process with adrenal fatigue. Shifting our expectations and learning to be patient are new survival skills clients have to develop, or their anxiety will overwhelm them and they'll return to drug and alcohol use. What rules you?

_____

_____

_____

_____

_____

_____

_____

_____

_____

"It was time to take the pumpkin out of the pot and eat it. In the final analysis, that was what solved these big problems of life. You could think and think and get nowhere, but you still had to eat your pumpkin. That brought you down to earth. That gave you a reason for going on. Pumpkin."

Alexander McCall Smith,
The No. 1 Ladies' Detective Agency

This is a wonderful reminder for those of us who have a tendency to overthink and complicate situations. We can wrack our brains and toss and turn, and ultimately we still need to eat our pumpkin. The basic routines we have in our lives keep us grounded. It's important to remember the simple self-care routines that include hygiene, meals, exercise and calling people who love waving at the neighbor as you leave. When you are working with a particularly tough cohort of clients at the center, it's a relief that you can still come home and read the paper, make a cup of tea, and sit in your favorite chair.

_____
_____
_____
_____
_____
_____
_____
_____
_____
_____

"It is hard to be angry when one has seen the sun rise," she said.
"It seems to be true," he admitted. "I wonder why.'"
"Because it makes one feel so small and insignificant. It has been rising forever and will rise forever no matter what we do or do not do. All our problems are as nothing to the sun."

David Gemmell, Sword in the Storm

Perspective is key for long term effectiveness as treatment providers. We can't get caught up in the politics and client chaos, and lose our ability to remember what really matters to us. This is easier said than done since our colleagues create another family dynamic for us, and we can have conflict and support just like we do with our family of origin. We can take their behavior personally, and forget that they were behaving the way they do way before they met us, and will be doing so well after leaving us. It can be a relief to remember how seldom it's about us.

_____

_____

_____

_____

_____

_____

_____

_____

_____

_____

"...we're told by TV and Reader's Digest that a crisis will trigger massive personal change--and that those big changes will make the pain worthwhile. But from what he could see, big change almost never happens. People simply feel lost. They have no idea what to say or do or feel or think. They become messes and tend to remain messes."

Douglas Coupland, The Gum Thief

We have certainly seen first-hand that crisis can bring clients through the doors, and most of the time they'll seem lost and indecisive about their next steps. This is natural because recovery was never Plan A. In fact, many of them are shocked to still be alive! When people are a mess they tend to be open in a way that they can't be otherwise. It creates a window of opportunity for us as helpers. We can help them rediscover themselves, and help them seek inward for their next steps, and create an ongoing structure that will be help sustain the changes they make.

"And this is the forbidden truth, the unspeakable taboo - that evil is not always repellent but frequently attractive; that it has the power to make of us not simply victims, as nature and accident do, but active accomplices."

Joyce Carol Oates

Of course this is true. Our treatment center is full of people who were initially attracted to the substance and lifestyle that eventually swallowed up their life. Not only were they not repelled, but they felt as though they had found a solution to the emptiness that plagued them. So, our drug of choice didn't find us, we found it. We just completely underestimated our vulnerability. We had the delusion that we could manage it. It's not just drugs. We enter unwise relationships, take sketchy employment, abuse our benefits . . . shifting our focus and definition of a satisfying life will be crucial. Some of our clients are more addicted to the criminal lifestyle than the drugs accompanying their using.

_____

_____

_____

_____

_____

_____

_____

_____

_____

_____

_____

December 1 — Empathy

"Were we incapable of empathy – of putting ourselves in the position of others and seeing that their suffering is like our own – then ethical reasoning would lead nowhere. If emotion without reason is blind, then reason without emotion is impotent."

Peter Singer, Writings on an Ethical Life

Empathy develops from accurate mirroring by our caretakers. When we have feelings they notice and address them. They even help us develop an emotional vocabulary by saying things like, "You look tired baby. Do you need a nap?" Or maybe, "You seem really angry right now." We learn to use words to express our internal world. If clients didn't receive this mirroring, they may be over-reliant on their intellect, and may not always read other people accurately. Teaching emotional intelligence skills is important for clients that struggle in this area. They need to practice social skills daily, and residential treatment is the perfect laboratory. We can give them the mirroring they need.

_____

_____

_____

_____

_____

_____

_____

_____

_____

"If you were born with the ability to change someone's perspective or emotions, never waste that gift. It is one of the most powerful gifts God can give—the ability to influence."

Shannon L. Alder

This truly is a gift, the gift of influence. As helpers we have the ability to sit quietly and provide a space for people to talk about their internal experience and actually HEAR themselves for the first time in a long time. We can guide them by pointing out their options and the consequences of each option. Ultimately, it will be up to them to choose their path. We can offer a calm, kind presence who can hear without judgment which is healing to those who've been judged. Some of us have carried this ability all of our lives and some of us have developed it as result of our own life experiences. Our lives softened us and helped us develop compassion or fellow suffers. No matter how you developed it, we are encouraged to treat our ability to influence as a gift.

_____
_____
_____
_____
_____
_____
_____
_____
_____
_____
_____

December 3 — Values

"What you do makes a difference, and you have to decide what kind of difference you want to make."

Jane Goodall

This is an interesting point and assumes that our actions affect others, regardless of the value of what we do. When we were using, we were affecting everyone we contacted. We left bad impressions, left chaos, left broken promises. When we get clean it reverses itself and we leave serenity, good communication, and honesty. What ı nice shift for the people in our world. But this is a choice we can make. We can choose how we are going to affect people and the kind of imprint we're going to leave on situations. This is an important message of hope for clients because they now have the option to change their impact on others through their sobriety. In the window of sobriety that treatment offers they can consider this and take stock of their values. The goal is for their life choices to match their values. How are you doing with this?

_____

_____

_____

_____

_____

_____

_____

_____

_____

_____

"If you treat an individual as he is, he will remain how he is. But if you treat him as if he were what he ought to be and could be, he will become what he ought to be and could be."

Johann Wolfgang von Goethe

I have always believed that we train people to treat us a particular way. When I had poor boundaries, people who have poor boundaries seem to find me like radar. They would take, I would give. When I began to respect myself, others in my life began to respect me. This exchange is important for helpers to keep in mind. If I treat the clients with suspicion and doubt, they are more likely to behave in suspicious and withholding ways. If I treat them with dignity and compassion they are more likely to be honest and forthcoming themselves. Is this always true? It's true that sometimes clients will mistake our kindness for weakness, which is ignorance on their part. It takes strength to treat people who lie to you with dignity.

_____

_____

_____

_____

_____

_____

_____

_____

_____

_____

_____

"When someone tells me "no," it doesn't mean I can't do it, it simply means I can't do it with them."

Karen E. Quinones Miller

When we become focused on a particular outcome, in a particular way, we develop blinders for other opportunities and options that might present themselves. For example, I want to be loved by someone that I've chosen and have become fixated on being with them. So when I'm blocked in some way I can become despairing, and even angry at God for not hearing me. It's important to surrender the outcome of what we need and want once we've done what we can. The path to meeting our heart-felt needs may be circular and less obvious that we would have predicted. It may take longer than we would have wanted. And we may need to shift our focus to include other people and other paths if we're going to get where we want to go. For example, maybe there's another way I will be loved.

_____

_____

_____

_____

_____

_____

_____

_____

_____

_____

"Do stuff. Be clenched, curious. Not waiting for inspiration's shove or society's kiss on your forehead. Pay attention. It's all about paying attention. Attention is vitality. It connects you with others. It makes you eager. Stay eager."

Susan Sontag

How awake are you in your own life? It's so easy to become comfortable with our routine and drift from one day to the next. It seems especially true the older you get! Now that I'm fifty time seems to roll downhill like a giant snowball! Staying alert to possibility and challenges make us participants in our lives instead of spectators. We ever know when something new will pop up, and it may be an indication that our life is about to change course. This can be exciting and provide us renewed energy and vitality. We can also initiate growth opportunities by signing up for interesting courses, networking with other professionals, and developing new skills. When was the last time you really challenged yourself? Maybe it's time.

_____

_____

_____

_____

_____

_____

_____

_____

_____

_____

_____

"The greatest disease in the West today is not TB or leprosy; it is being unwanted, unloved, and uncared for. We can cure physical diseases with medicine, but the only cure for loneliness, despair, and hopelessness is love. There are many in the world who are dying for a piece of bread but there are many more dying for a little love. The poverty in the West is a different kind of poverty -- it is not only a poverty of loneliness but also of spirituality. There's a hunger for love, as there is a hunger for God."

Mother Teresa, A Simple Path: Mother Teresa

I had read this before, and when I came across it again I was reminded of how touched I was the first time. It felt intuitively right. We see this with our clients all the time. They may have many resources or none, but they have a hole in their heart. Drugs, sex, crime, relationships couldn't fill it. It's a profound need to belong to something greater than the self- to be part of the human race as a welcome member. We can welcome them into treatment as desired guests.

_____

_____

_____

_____

_____

_____

_____

_____

_____

_____

_____

"Our wounds are often the openings into the best and most beautiful part of us."

David Richo

Sometimes our image of ourselves needs to break to a million pieces for there to be room for new parts of us to emerge. Managing our image takes a lot time and energy because we're so heavily invested in keeping it. It can take something truly devastating to let it slip from our grasp, and we're left fully exposed. Then something horrific happens. We're arrested, our partner leaves us, or we're diagnosed with a serious illness and our image can't help us. There's an opportunity here if we can see it. As helpers, we can help our clients see the opportunity that their situation provides them. Technically this is called a "reframe" but it also happens to be a spiritual opening. Our wounds often led us to become helpers, and they are why we can be especially compassionate and patient.

_____

_____

_____

_____

_____

_____

_____

_____

_____

_____

_____

"People take different roads seeking fulfillment and happiness. Just because they're not on your road doesn't mean they've gotten lost."

Dalai Lama XIV

Recovering staff sometimes struggle with allegiance to the way they got clean and sober. If they got and remained clean through a religious organization, they feel pulled toward recommending that path to other addicts. If they got clean in NA or AA, they feel the same compulsion to guide clients toward the fellowship. It can be tough to set aside our conviction that our way is THE way because it may have saved our life. However, recovering helpers need to become more pragmatic, and be attached to making recommendation that clients will actually follow. That means becoming familiar with alternatives like local support groups not affiliated with the Twelve Steps, or Celebrate Recovery through the church. It doesn't matter how someone stays clean. It matters that they have a chance to do so.

_____

_____

_____

_____

_____

_____

_____

_____

_____

_____

December 10 — Attraction not promotion

"I never liked jazz music because jazz music doesn't resolve. But I was outside the Bagdad Theater in Portland one night when I saw a man playing the saxophone. I stood there for fifteen minutes, and he never opened his eyes.
After that I liked jazz music.
Sometimes you have to watch somebody love something before you can love it yourself. It is as if they are showing you the way."

Donald Miller, Blue Like Jazz: Nonreligious Thoughts on Christian Spirituality

Recovery is also most effective when it is sought out by attraction and not promotion. When people see recovering folks living a good life, a joyful full life, they get a glimmer of hope. Recovering staff serve as role models for what might be possible for clients who make a decision to change their lives. Would somebody want what you have? Do YOU want what you have?

_____

_____

_____

_____

_____

_____

_____

_____

_____

_____

_____

"Anger ... it's a paralyzing emotion ... you can't get any-thing done. People sort of think it's an interesting, passion-ate, and igniting feeling — I don't think it's any of that — it's helpless ... it's absence of control — and I need all of my skills, all of the control, all of my powers ... and anger doesn't provide any of that — I have no use for it whatso-ever."
[Interview with CBS radio host Don Swaim, September 15, 1987.]

Toni Morrison

A lot of our clients believe that they are most power-ful, most in control when they are angry. They prefer anger to sadness, so are quick to become angry when beginning to feel vulnerable. If we aren't careful, the energy that we can get from anger can begin to con-trol and drive us places we never intended to go. It can make our hearts race, our breathing shallow, and we can even feel our chest get tighter. Over the long term, we can experience considerable physical and emotional pain when our anger isn't moderated. Our sobriety depends on it.

_____

_____

_____

_____

_____

_____

_____

_____

December 12 — Whining

"Whining is not only graceless, but can be dangerous. It can alert a brute that a victim is in the neighborhood."

Maya Angelou, Wouldn't Take Nothing for
My Journey Now

This is a fabulous quote. Some of our clients are professional whiners, and we do see them exploited in the treatment center by other clients. It's easy. Other clients' just need to complain a lot in front of a whiner, and pretty soon the whiner will do the complaining for them, while the instigators gets to sit back and just watch what happens. As annoying as whining clients can be to us, they are also vulnerable to other more manipulative if not sociopathic clients. We need to work with them to use their voice more effectively, and develop social skills such as conflict resolution. Sometimes the whiner is a co-worker, and this can get to us on a daily basis. Remember it's a sign of powerlessness, so you need patience.

"We must assume every event has significance and contains a message that pertains to our questions...this especially applies to what we used to call bad things...the challenge is to find the silver lining in every event, no matter how negative."

James Redfield, The Celestine Prophecy

What do you think about this perspective? It can be hard to hold this thought when we are in the middle of the fog. Our clients are facing some harsh realities once they get clean, some more frightening than others. While it would not be helpful to say "I'm sure this is for the best," we can suggest the possibility that the situation opens up new options that may not have been available otherwise. When something ends, something else is now free to begin. Maybe it's time to recognize a multi-generational pattern that can now be broken. Maybe our marriage really does need to end, or we need a new job and we've been too frighten to initiate the needed change ourselves. Time will tell.

_____

_____

_____

_____

_____

_____

_____

_____

_____

_____

"Do you understand how amazing it is to hear that from an adult? Do you know how amazing it is to hear that from anybody? It's one of the simplest sentences in the world, just four words, but they're the four hugest words in the world when they're put together. You can do it."

Sherman Alexie, The Absolutely True Diary of a Part-Time Indian

Some of our clients have never heard these words in their life In fact, their childhood was spent hearing the opposite: "You can't do it," "You'll never be anything," or "You're worthless." As staff in the recovery center we have the opportunity to be the voice that says, "Yes you can," "Yes, you matter," and "You're welcome here." Our clients are deeply shamed-based, and are hungry for support, approval and forgiveness. They need nonjudgmental acceptance and recognition for the talents and strengths they bring. It's a joy to give it.

_____

_____

_____

_____

_____

_____

_____

_____

_____

_____

_____

_____

DECEMBER 15 — ENTITLEMENT

"The more invested I am in my own ideas about reality, the more those experiences will feel like victimizations rather than the ups and downs of relating. Actually, I believe that the less I conceptualize things that way, the more likely it is that people will want to stay by me, because they will not feel burdened, consciously or unconsciously, by my projections, judgments, entitlements, or unrealistic expectations."

David Richo, Daring to Trust: Opening Ourselves to Real Love and Intimacy

This is a powerful message. When my worldview is entitlement and expectation it's a set up for frustration and disappointment. We see this in the treatment center all the time. Clients who feel very entitled to exceptions because of the program fees paid by their family; or criminal justice clients who feel that they've got something coming. Then there's others who feel like life has been grossly unfair to them, so they are owed something by the world. We can share with our clients the principle that you receive what you put in, so ante up!

_____

_____

_____

_____

_____

_____

_____

_____

_____

DECEMBER 16 — ROLE MODELS

"Some want to live within the sound
Of church or chapel bell;
I want to run a rescue shop,
Within a yard of hell."

C.T. Studd

When I read this I thought of those who choose to work within the criminal justice system. Maybe they deliver treatment in incarcerated settings, maybe they work with parolees, or maybe they train alcohol and drug counselors who are serving life sentences. Some people have a tremendous heart for this population, I would even say calling, to meet these clients in very difficult settings. It's not pleasant to hear doors slam behind you, or face the disgruntled expression on a CO's face who thinks programs like ours pose a security threat and are bogus. We have to be willing to deliver the services around lock downs and disruptions. This is our chance to be role models of recovery as clients watch us work our way through the politics of incarceration with grace.

_____

_____

_____

_____

_____

_____

_____

_____

_____

_____

"MANAGE YOUR MOOD: Name 1 thing that surprised you today...Name 1 thing that moved you...Name 1 thing that inspired you..."

Gino Norris

This is a marvelous formula! This formula shifts our perspective toward awareness. We are reminded to recognize that we're affected by our interactions with the world and other people. This would actually be a good way to start a group check in or maybe an exercise for family group. It would be a good practice for our clients to use this formula to manage their moods. How about you? I decided to do this myself:

I was surprised by an unexpected invitation to Thanksgiving.

I was moved by the emotional honesty of the women in a meeting.

I was inspired when I ran across an old project when preparing for a workshop.

"You are blessed today not because God loves you most but, God just want to bless someone through you. So just be careful you might probably be holding onto someone's blessings. Remember you are just servant/messenger of God."

wisdom kavi

This is a beautiful reminder to remember that we are channels for healing and not the source of healing. We are the arms and legs of a Higher Power and we have the ability to deliver the needed hug of encouragement and patient ear when they are acting out. We can deliver the unconditional regard that the clients and co-workers around us need, and we can accept the same from someone else. We never know when our presence will and words will be exactly what is needed for someone to have a breakthrough they were never expecting. Sometimes I've said things I thought were fairly ordinary only to be told later that the person thought about it all night and it change their outlook. Lucky us.

_____

_____

_____

_____

_____

_____

_____

_____

_____

_____

December 19 — Support

"If you've just left a place of difficulty, don't then move into the shadows, alone with your thoughts. Spend your time with friends, or even just people who care about you. It might feel more self-protective to isolate yourself, but the reality is that you need to let the light in."

Sally Hanan

The desire to retreat and stay in the shadows is so human when we feel defeated and alienated. Our clients have spent years operating in the shadows, disappearing for long periods for time and even hiding from themselves. As they come out into the light they may squint a little, feel a little shy about revealing themselves, and we can support their emersion from the darkness by being welcoming and curious about them. Some of us still struggle with the desire to isolate and have to be coaxed out to meetings and the occasional lunch by people who love us. We can extend compassion to the client who are squinting in the light, and see them as a reminder of how much courage recovery requires.

_____

_____

_____

_____

_____

_____

_____

_____

_____

_____

_____

"Fear and anxiety many times indicates that we are moving in a positive direction, out of the safe confines of our comfort zone, and in the direction of our true purpose."

Charles F. Glassman, Brain Drain The Breakthrough That Will Change Your Life

This is such a helpful perspective on anxiety! Anxiety is not to be avoided, in fact, existentialists see it as a valuable impetus to push us forward. It's a sign we're out of our safe zone and maybe taking the risks we need to practice new behaviors. Our clients are frequently anxious, and as a helpers we can remind them of the growing pains that come when they wake back up after a long drug-induced sleep. We can help clients figure out the where they want to go in sobriety, and then create a plan to develop the skills they'll need to practice while they're with us that will help them be successful when they leave treatment. We can practice with them today.

"...everybody, every single person, has a story to tell. Every single ordinary person has an extraordinary story. We might all think that we are unremarkable, that our lives are boring, just because we aren't doing ground-breaking things or making headlines or winning awards. But the truth is we all do something that is fascinating, that is brave, that is something we should proud of."

Cecelia Ahern, Irish Girls Are Back in Town

I've heard clients worry that their story is "boring," and missing the drama that other recovering people may have experienced. Maybe they had a high bottom, so still have their families or jobs and have never been arrested. It's only in the recovery world that these things might be a point of embarrassment! Our choice to work in recovery is shaped by our choices in life. Who we are is actually our best therapeutic tool. We are enhanced with the clinical skills we learned in school, but our compassion, sense of humor and perspective are a result of our life experiences. You are enough, I promise.

_____

_____

_____

_____

_____

_____

_____

_____

_____

_____

DECEMBER 22 — LIVING ON PURPOSE

"It's humbling to start fresh. It takes a lot of courage. But it can be reinvigorating. You just have to put your ego on a shelf & tell it to be quiet."

Jennifer Ritchie Payette

When clients lose everything and have to start over, so many opportunities can open for them. They're no longer trapped by the choices they've made – their life has been demolished and they get to choose a new one. It's hard to see this situation as an opportunity because it can feel so devastating. As helpers, we can offer this perspective. Maybe we've even started over ourselves, so can have empathy for how daunting it can look. It starts with learning enough about themselves that they can begin to make choices about their career, their friendships, where they want to live, and the kind of people they want to date in sobriety. The key is to choose not to react, which is how most addicts have lived their lives. They have the chance to live their life ON PURPOSE.

_____

_____

_____

_____

_____

_____

_____

_____

_____

_____

"There is something infantile in the presumption that somebody else has a responsibility to give your life meaning and point... The truly adult view, by contrast, is that our life is as meaningful, as full and as wonderful as we choose to make it."

R. Dawkins, The Blind Watchmaker

Some of us have spent so much of our life wanting someone unavailable to love us, and believe that if they would do so we could finally be happy. And, of course, if they're unavailable so they never do. So, we're never happy. Maybe our addiction started to manage the longing that never seemed to get met. Alcoholics Anonymous talks about emotional maturity as part of recovery, and one of the signs of emotional maturity is to recognize that we are responsible for our happiness. We can choose people in our lives that contribute to our happiness or our misery, but it is still our choice. This is the GOOD news - we have more power and influence in our lives than we knew which means there's genuine hope for change. We really can be happy.

"Want to keep Christ in Christmas? Feed the hungry, clothe the naked, forgive the guilty, welcome the unwanted, care for the ill, love your enemies, and do unto others as you would have done unto you."

Steve Maraboli, Unapologetically You: Reflections on Life and the Human Experience

This hit me between the eyes as profoundly true. It's Christmas time as I write this and I'm surrounded by the commercial frenzy. It can be exhausting. The spirit of the season can be expressed in other ways, ways suggested in the quote above. We can extend the spirit in our work with clients, some of whom haven't had a peaceful or joyful holiday season in many years. Maybe they're usually incarcerated this time of year, or in the homeless shelter. We can offer simple decorations in the facility, maybe a small token for each client under the tree. We can encourage family to visit on Christmas tomorrow as we operate under our holiday schedule. We can be family for those without family.

"Then the Grinch thought of something he hadn't before!
What if Christmas, he thought, doesn't come from a store.
What if Christmas...perhaps...means a little bit more!"

Dr. Seuss, How the Grinch Stole Christmas!

Merry Christmas. Happy Hanukkah. Happy Kwanzaa . . . This is a magical time of the year. If you're working today, you are doing something important with your time even if you can't be with your family today. You will be part of creating a meaningful and peaceful day for people who sorely need this experience. Maybe you're single, so you always get holiday duty so people with kids can have the day off. If that's you, I challenge you to take the day off next year, even if you spend it with your pet. You can have a holiday too. Visitation today may be awkward for the families, and when they leave the clients may have feelings about being left behind. Your presence will be comforting and stabilizing today. Thank you for your service!

_____

_____

_____

_____

_____

_____

_____

_____

_____

_____

"I was giving up. I would have given up - if a voice hadn't made itself heard in my heart. The voice said "I will not die. I refuse it. I will make it through this nightmare. I will beat the odds, as great as they are. I have survived so far, miraculously. Now I will turn miracle into routine. The amazing will be seen everyday. I will put in all the hard work necessary. Yes, so long as God is with me, I will not die. Amen."

Yann Martel, Life of Pi

Our clients are resilient survivors. Some of them have evaded death more than once between overdoses and violence. It's a miracle they're still here, and they're just as surprised to be alive as anyone. There's something in them that has kept them fighting to live despite their self-destructive efforts. Recovery offers them the chance to live intentionally instead of accidentally We're in a position to help them weigh the pros and cons of choosing to live and then creating a plan to make this possible. Miracles DO happen.

"I learned to love the fool in me. The one who feels too much, talks too much, takes too many chances, wins sometimes & loses often, lacks self-control, loves & hates, hurts & gets hurt, promises & breaks promises, laughs & cries."

Theodore Isaac Rubin

How are you doing coming to terms with the foolish, bungling, blurting, inelegant part of you? We all have these parts, so we have to work them through. Otherwise, we spend so much of our time denying them and creating defenses to cover them up. Even when we do our inventories and ask for our defects to be removed they don't disappear – they can be transformed into useful traits under the right situations. For example, losing allows us to still be teachable. Hurting allows us to receive support and encouragement. Laughter draws people close to us and lowers our walls. We need all the parts of us to be a whole person, and to connect with other people. "Our weaknesses bind us, not our strengths" says Ernst Koontz.

_____
_____
_____
_____
_____
_____
_____
_____
_____
_____

"Our lives are part of a unique adventure... Nevertheless, most of us think the world is 'normal' and are constantly hunting for something abnormal--like angels or Martians. But that is just because we don't realize the world is a mystery. As for myself, I felt completely different. I saw the world as an amazing dream. I was hunting for some kind of explanation of how everything fit together."

Jostein Gaarder, The Solitaire Mystery

It's easy to miss the small miracles that happen all around us. We live in a highly stimulating world which takes our focus to the outside world on a daily basis. One of our vantage points as a counselor is to be able to see patterns and themes in the stories our clients share with us. We can see how one decision led to another decision, and how the fabric of their lives hangs together. This perspective is invaluable to clients because it reminds them that the choices they have made have still taken them forward, even if it has been a crooked road.

_____

_____

_____

_____

_____

_____

_____

_____

_____

_____

DECEMBER 29 — LIVING OUR VALUES

"The philosopher Diogenes was eating bread and lentils for supper. He was seen by the philosopher Aristippus, who lived comfortably by flattering the king. Said Aristippus, 'If you would learn to be subservient to the king you would not have to live on lentils.'

Said Diogenes, 'Learn to live on lentils and you will not have to be subservient to the king".'

Anthony de Mello

Who do you serve? Maybe Visa? The bank that holds your mortgage? Our stuff can begin to take over our lives, and we find ourselves working very hard to maintain our lifestyle, much like treading water. We take on extra jobs or shifts that we are truthfully too tired to manage. Our health and our families suffer. Maybe if we did with a little less "stuff" we would have more time? It's something to think about. Life can be simpler than we make it.

DECEMBER 30 — HOPE

"The thing about being catapulted into a whole new life--or at least, shoved up so hard against someone else's life that you might as well have your face pressed against their window--is that it forces you to rethink your idea of who you are. Or how you might seem to other people."

Jojo Moyes, Me Before You

Many of our clients landed back into reality pretty hard. They feel shoved against a wall, maybe even through a wall, so they can be tender and reactive. They are forced to reconsider their life trajectory, and make some hard decisions. Choosing sobriety can seem like a much harder decision than continuing to have consequences, because most of their skill sets are created to manage the consequences. We have the chance to offer them hope for change, and belief in their own competence should they choose change. Only the clients will know when they are "sick and tired of being sick and tired."

_____

_____

_____

_____

_____

_____

_____

_____

_____

_____

_____

December 31 — Perspective

"In the autumn of your years don't make it so that what you look back on is regret. Live your life now so that whatever you do gives some sunshine before you head into the winter of your life."

Stephen Richards

As we close out this year, it's a time to reflect on the past 12 months, and look forward to the next year. We've made some really good clinical interventions and handled a lot of crisis. We have also let ourselves get too tired sometimes, and lost our perspective. New Year's Eve resolutions have never been particularly useful for me, but it can be helpful to remember that the goals is to get to the end of your life with as few regrets as possible. When you think about the decisions coming up in the next few months, consider them from the future vantage point, and avoid "If only's", and "I should have's" whenever possible. Life is precious.

If you wish to contact Mary please feel free to call, send an email, or write to:

Mary Crocker Cook
1710 Hamilton Ave. #8
San Jose, CA 95125.

Phone: (408) 448-0333

Email:
marycook@connectionscounselingassociates.com

For more information about Mary's counseling services or presentation topics visit:

www.marycrockercook.com

CPSIA information can be obtained
at www.ICGtesting.com
Printed in the USA
FSOW01n0710070515
6971FS